THE INDIAN JUNGLE

THE INDIAN JUNGLE
Psychoanalysis and Non-Western Civilizations

Sudhir Kakar

First published in 2024 by
Karnac Books Limited
62 Bucknell Road
Bicester
Oxfordshire OX26 2DS

British Library Cataloguing in Publication Data

A C.I.P. for this book is available from the British Library

ISBN: 978-1-91556-520-4 (paperback)
ISBN: 978-1-91556-518-1 (e-book)

Typeset by vPrompt eServices Pvt Ltd, India

Printed in the United Kingdom

www.firingthemind.com

*I shall now try with your guidance to penetrate into the Indian jungle
from which until now an uncertain blending of Hellenic love of
proportion, Jewish sobriety, and Philistine timidity have kept me away.
I really ought to have tackled it earlier, for the plants of this soil shouldn't
be alien to me; I have dug to certain depths for their roots. But it isn't
easy to pass beyond the limits of one's nature.*

—Sigmund Freud to Romain Rolland, January 19, 1930.
Letters, pp. 292–293

For my granddaughter Elsie, a writer in the making

Contents

Acknowledgments

I wish to thank the Hans Kilian and Lotte Köhler Centre at the University of Bochum for the award of the Lotte Köhler Prize for Psychoanalytic Developmental, Cultural and Social Psychology, 2022 that encouraged me to write this book.

With the exception of the Introduction, some of the material in these essays first appeared in journal articles that have been revised and considerably expanded for this book.

Chapter 1 is a revised and expanded version of "Culture and Psychoanalysis. A Personal Journey," *Social Analysis*, *50*(2), 2006.

Chapter 2 is a revised and expanded version of "The Maternal-Feminine in Indian Psychoanalysis," *International Review of Psychoanalysis*, *16*(3), 1989.

Chapter 3 is a revised and expanded version of "Psychoanalysis and Eastern Healing Traditions," *Journal of Analytical Psychology*, *48*, 2003.

Chapter 4 is a revised and expanded version of "Psyche and Nature: Notes from the Indian Terroir," *Psychoanalysis, Culture & Society* (in press).

Chapter 5 is a revised and expanded version of "Last Claims: Sexuality and Sexual Imagination in Old Age," *Psychoanalytic Quarterly*, 88(4): 813–837, 2019, DOI: 10.1080/00332828.2019.1651609, copyright © The Psychoanalytic Quarterly 2019, reprinted by permission of Taylor & Francis Ltd, https://www.tandfonline.com on behalf of *The Psychoanalytic Quarterly*.

About the author

Sudhir Kakar is an Indian psychoanalyst and writer. He has been a lecturer and visiting professor at Harvard University, visiting professor at the universities of Chicago, McGill, Melbourne, Hawaii, and Vienna, fellow at the Institutes of Advanced Study, Princeton, Berlin, and Cologne, and is on the board of the Freud Archives.

His many honors include the Kardiner Award of Columbia University, the Boyer Prize for Psychological Anthropology of the American Anthropological Association, the Tagore-Merck Award, the Lotte Köhler Prize for Psychoanalytic Developmental, Cultural and Social Psychology, the Distinguished Service Award of the Indo-American Psychiatric Association, India's Bhabha, Nehru, and ICSSR National Fellowships, Germany's Goethe Medal, McArthur Research Fellowship, and the Order of Merit of the Federal Republic of Germany, the country's highest civilian honor. As "the psychoanalyst of civilizations," the French weekly *Le Nouvel Observateur* listed Kakar in 2005 as one of the world's twenty-five major thinkers.

Kakar is the author of fourteen books of non-fiction and six novels. His books have been translated into twenty languages around the world. Learn more at his website: www.sudhirkakar.com.

Introduction

What psychoanalysis is possible in a traditional non-Western society like India with its characteristic family system, religious beliefs, and cultural values? Is the mental life of non-Western patients radically different from that of their Western counterparts? Over the years, in my own talks to diverse audiences in India, Europe, and the United States, these two questions have invariably constituted the core of animated discussion.

We have to ask them, because most of our knowledge on how human beings feel, think, act is derived from a small subset of the human population. Since 2010, following psychologist Joseph Heinrich and colleagues, we have called this subset the WEIRD, now famously Western, Educated, Industrialized, Rich, and Democratic. This small group of statistical outliers are both the producers and subjects of the contemporary psychological knowledge that we have then blithely proceeded to generalize to the rest of humankind.

The WEIRD, for instance, have a distinctive morality. The chasm that divides WEIRD morality from others is observed in a 2012 experiment by social psychologist Jonathan Haidt who studied morality in twelve groups of different social classes in different countries. During his interviews, Haidt would tell the interviewee stories, and he then asks if there is something wrong in how someone acts in the story and, if so, why. One of the stories goes: A man goes to the supermarket once a week and buys a chicken. But before cooking the chicken, he has sexual intercourse with it. Then he cooks it and eats it.

Only one group out of the twelve showed a majority (73 percent) who tolerated the chicken story, finding it acceptable. These were students from the University of Pennsylvania, a liberal, Ivy League college in the United States and certainly the most WEIRD among the twelve selected groups. Their rationale for their tolerance: "It's his chicken, it's dead, nobody is getting hurt and it's being done in private" (Haidt, 2012, loc. 184).

Like other large groups, such as the major non-Western civilizations, the WEIRDs have a distinctive cultural imagination that attended the birth of psychoanalysis and continues to pervade its theories and models.[1] Seeded into a network of minds, we absorb our cultural imagination and its worldview from early on in life—not via the logic of the head, but via the emotional stirrings of the heart and body in which this imagination is encoded. Our cultural imagination shapes what Roy Schaefer (1970) called "vision of reality" that is not a set of philosophical doctrines, relevant only for religious and intellectual elites, but beliefs bordering on convictions, many of them unconscious, that are reflected in the lives, songs, and stories of a vast number of people who share a common culture. It is the culture's vision of reality that interprets central human experiences and answers perennial questions on what is good and what is evil, what is real and what is unreal, what is the essential nature of men and women and the world they live in, and what is a person's connection to nature, to other human beings, and to the cosmos. A civilization's vision of reality plays a significant role even in how it organizes knowledge, how it shapes the processes of attention, perception, reasoning, and inference making. For instance, research into cognitive processes since the 1960s (Segall et al., 1966) shows that perception is strongly influenced by cultural differences

---

[1] For better readability, I will henceforth use the term "Western" for WEIRD. Although the cultures of psychoanalysis in South America, France, Italy, England, United States, and so on have distinct and important differences, they all share a strong family resemblance that distinguishes them clearly from the cultural imaginations of Indian, Chinese, Japanese, and other non-Western civilizations.

(Nisbett & Miyamoto, 2005). Commenting on cultural variations in perception in the Müller–Lyer illusion where lines of equal length give impressions of different length, an illusion created by the orientation of the arrow caps placed at their ends, Alfred Margulies (2014) observes:

> our cultural environment in its everyday structures, practices and aesthetics shapes the way our brains process visual information. And, if this is true for neurobiological non-conscious visual processing, it seems almost certain it would be true for psychoanalytically relevant unconscious processes and the impact of culture. (p. 5)

Indeed, if the ego is a skin ego, dependent upon the physical body to find its mental representation, then does the early life of skin—shaped, after all, by culture—impact how ego gets constructed in different cultural contexts (Kakar & Narayanan, 2023)? We might wonder whether ego formation is different in India where urban-area breastfeeding we are told (UNICEF, 2018) continues for over a year for children of both genders, at a rate of 79 percent, compared to the United States where extended breastfeeding rates are around 6.2 percent. From breastfeeding, the Indian child proceeds not to spoon-feeding but to hand-feeding, less frequently to strollers than to being carried on the mother's side or back in skin contact, and extended co-sleeping with parents or elder relatives. In this atmosphere of early life, conveyed by visible skin contact over a long period, it would be reasonable to expect that the account of mental life in infancy would not exactly hew to the reigning psychoanalytic models derived from Western experience.

The mental representations of culture, our cultural imagination, has been a relatively unexplored territory in psychoanalytic discourse. Disseminated through myths and legends, proverbs and metaphors, iconic artworks, the stories a society's members tell each other, enacted in rituals, conveyed through tales told to children, given a modern veneer in films, the cultural imagination is equally glimpsed in admonitions of parents, in the future vistas they hold out to their children, indeed even in the way their children are touched and fed and carried about.

For more than a century, the cultural imagination of psychoanalysis has been assumed and largely continues to be assumed as being Western. Fundamental ideas about human relationships, family, marriage, and gender that are essentially cultural in origin often remain unexamined as if they are shared by analyst and patient alike. Though these fundamental ideas belong to WEIRD culture, they pervade the analytic space as if they were universally valid. Thus ideas that are historically and culturally only true of and limited to modern Western—specifically European and North American middle class—experience are incorporated unquestioned into psychoanalytic theory.

With the rise of relativism in the human sciences and politically with the advent of decolonization in the second half of the twentieth century, human sciences took a sceptic turn, to which psychoanalysis has not been immune. Intellectually, the relativistic position owes much of its impetus to Foucault's powerful argument on the rootedness of all thought in history and culture—and in the framework of power relations. Adherents of this perspective are not a priori willing to accept why psychoanalysis, a product of early twentieth-century European bourgeois family and social structure, should be an exception to the general rule on the incapacity of thought to transcend its roots. In the intellectual climate of our times, then, the cultural and historical transcendence of psychoanalytic theories can no longer be taken for granted.

For a long time—up to a few decades ago—psychoanalysis was reluctant to accord culture a defining role in the construction of individual subjectivity. In the various phases of its encounter with anthropology, which could conceivably have tempered its Western-cultural orientation, psychoanalysis has taken a privileged, asymmetric position in its relationship with anthropology: there has been psychoanalytical anthropology but not an anthropological psychoanalysis. Analysts have continued to regard ethnographic facts and the methods used to uncover them as belonging to the "surface" of human behavior and hence superficial; they are not considered "deep" enough to merit the respectful attention given to the reports of practicing analysts. The few anthropologists among analysts—especially the pioneers of the psychoanalytic anthropology such as Géza Róheim (1950) and George Devereux—reinforced the privileged position of psychoanalysis by applying psychoanalytic concepts to cultures, almost as if the former were a fixed set of tools, rather than a means of making analysts more culturally sensitive and reflective. According to Devereux (1978), for instance, any doubts about a universal, a-cultural conception of psychoanalysis were to be rigorously combated. For him, analysis was a science independent of all cultural thought models and any efforts to "reculturalize" it were to be strongly resisted; a psychoanalysis with cultural connotations would no longer be a science but merely one of the myths of the occidental world. All that Devereux was willing to grant was the presence of an ethnic unconscious built from a specific constellation of defense mechanisms that a given culture brings to bear on human experience, and through which the necessary renunciation of universal wishes and fantasies can be achieved.

Despite these obstacles, the rise of the multicultural movement in many Western societies has resulted in more and more calls from analysts of varying persuasions in many different countries (Bergeret, 1993; Davidson, 1988; Rendon, 1993; Yampey, 1989) to re-examine the issue of culture in psychoanalysis and not shy away from any "reculturalization" if found necessary. Indeed, the intersection of psychoanalysis, culture, and society has been called the new frontier in psychoanalytic theorizing (Ainslie, 2018). Salman Akhtar (2008, 2009), for instance, has been a pioneer in bringing contributions from Muslim and East Asian societies, otherwise at the "periphery" of psychoanalytic discourse, to the attention of the Western "metropolis." Yet, given the dominant social concerns of Western societies, it is the cultures of race and class, rather than those of a society or even a civilization, that continue to draw most psychoanalytic attention (e.g., Altman, 1995, 2000; Dalal, 2002, 2006; Layton, 2006).

My argument against psychoanalysis as a universal enterprise where "one size fits all" rather than as a global one that reflects cultural nuances does not mean that I subscribe to an extreme culturally relativist position. Cultural conditions cannot by themselves account for intrapsychic constellations or even the behavior of individuals in a given culture. Nor do I share the postmodernist belief that there is no essential human nature at all. I would resist the notion of the person as a *tabula rasa* without "innate" desires, wishes, and fantasies although recognizing that one may differ about the basis of this innateness being biology, universal conditions of human infancy, or a combination of the two. A person is greatly modifiable but not infinitely so, with a mental life that is the end product of a complex interaction between the person's culture, family milieu, and his or her own needs and desire-based fantasies.

In another, more dynamic formulation to which I would subscribe, the individual self is a system of reverberating representational worlds—representations of his culture, primary family relationships, and bodily life—each enriching, constraining, and shaping the others as they jointly evolve through the life cycle (J. M. Ross, 1994). None of these constituting inner worlds (imaginations of body, family, and culture) are "primary" or "deeper"; all of them flow into the same river we call the psyche. There is thus no need for a hierarchical ordering of aspects of the psyche or to attempt an "archaeological" layering of the different inner worlds, although at different times the self may well be primarily experienced in one or the other representational mode.

To put this in Freudian language, the reality of the reality principle which the ego endeavors to substitute for the pleasure principle of the id is essentially cultural. The cultural reality I engage with in this book of essays, a sequel to an earlier collection (Kakar, 1997) is primarily Hindu-Indian, even as I am aware that an individual Indian's cultural imagination is modified by the specific cultures of their family, caste, class, or ethnic group. Yet even in the modern Hindu-Indian, who forms the bulk of the clientele for psychoanalytic therapy in the metropolises of Delhi, Mumbai, Bengaluru, and Kolkata, one finds that the Indian civilizational heritage has not disappeared from their psyche. Just as we talk about an intergenerational transmission of trauma, we need to be aware of a preconscious and unconscious intergenerational transmission of culture. The modern Indian of the future, too, will continue to have an ancient heart.

The Indian journey of psychoanalysis begins with Girindrasekhar Bose, the founder and the longtime president of the Indian Psychoanalytical Society who linked Indian philosophical thought with psychoanalysis even as he produced original work on the cultural moments in his patients' mental life in essays for the newly founded journal of the Indian Psychoanalytical Society (Bose, 1948, 1949, 1950). As early as 1929, Bose, perhaps the first analyst to raise the issue of cultural relativity of some of psychoanalytic propositions, wrote to Freud: "Indian patients do not exhibit castration symptoms to such a marked degree as my European cases," and "The desire to be female is more easily unearthed in Indian male patients than in

European", and "The Oedipus mother is very often a combined parental image" (Sinha, 1966).

Freud was politely dismissive of this challenge from Calcutta to the psychoanalytic claim of universality of its theories and models, especially the Oedipus complex, and the discussion did not go further.[2] Privately, he showed some irritation with Bose and the first generation of Indian analysts. For instance, he is reported to have remarked to his patient, the poet Hilda Doolittle (1956), "On the whole, I think my Indian students have reacted in the least satisfactory way to my teaching" (p. 68). And later, in the context of the Japanese Association, the only other non-Western society in the IPA at the time, H.D. writes (Friedman, 1981): "He [Freud] and I agreed that the Jap may be something where the Hindoo was all muddles with unconscious and with psychoanalysis in general" (p. 320). And when analyzing the writer Mulkraj Anand, who went to see Freud for a few sessions in Vienna as a young man, Freud burst out mid-session: "You Indians, with your eternal mother-complex!" (Kakar, 1995).

As I have observed earlier (Kakar, 1997), like sexist discourse, which either looks down at women as whores or elevates them to goddesses, colonial psychoanalytical discourse also dismissed non-Western people

> either as irrational, less-differentiated primitives or elevated them to a class of noble savages, close to unconscious rhythms of life and nature and possessors of an intuitive wisdom. Whereas Freud can be said to exemplify the former tendency, Jung is clearly the representative of the latter; both were part of their colonial times and were influenced by the European hegemonic ideology. (p. 31)

Freud's world (as also Jung's) was still that of a colonial Europe, which regarded itself as the center of the world, culturally, intellectually, and politically. It was a world untouched by the globalization and decolonization of our times, and it is unfair to expect that Freud should be an

---

[2] Three years later, Freud showed similar disinterest in "the father of Japanese psychoanalysis" Heisaku Kosawa's theory of the Ajase complex in Japan which he contrasted with the Oedipus complex (Okinogi, 2009).

exception who transcends the rule of rootedness of thought in culture and history.

The colonial mindset was particularly crass in the writings of British analysts claiming a close familiarity with Hindu-Indian culture and society. C. D. Daly, an officer in the British Indian army who was one of the twelve founding members of the Indian Psychoanalytical Society in 1922, published a paper in the *International Journal of Psychoanalysis*, where he wrote that "the Hindu people would have to make an effort to overcome their infantile and feminine tendencies ... The role of the British Government should be that of wise parents" (Hartnack, 2001, p. 67).

Owen Berkeley Hill (1921), a psychiatrist in the Indian Medical Corps and the other British founder-member of the Indian Society, attributed to Hindus an anal-erotic character, asserting that Hindus do not have a psychological disposition for leadership and thus need to be ruled. In addition to being obsessive–compulsive, they were also infantile, since "their general level of thought partakes of the variety usually peculiar to children" (Hartnack, 2001, p. 52).

The colonial mindset of pathologizing a non-Western people in even its most reputed professional journals by analysts without a claim to a serious engagement with and understanding of Indian civilization lingered on far into the 1980s.[3]

Well into the 1940s, work of Indian analysts around Bose, not easily available to Western colleagues, shows a persisting concern with the illumination of Indian cultural phenomena as well the "Indian" aspects of their patients' mental life (Kakar, 1997). After Bose's death in 1953, cultural critique receded from psychoanalytical awareness, even among Indian analysts (Kakar, 1997). In the last three decades,

---

[3] For instance, Nathaniel Ross, the coeditor of the *Journal of the American Psychoanalytic Association*, observes (1975): "I am afraid that the Hindu striving toward Nirvana may well be related to the terrible failures and cruelties of this culture (as the appalling prevalence of abysmal poverty, the infantile death rate, the infamous caste system, with its ugly notion of 'the untouchables,' the dismal failure to control overpopulation) and the dangers of escapism implicit in a too unworldly approach to life" (p. 90).

Or, in almost a caricature of psychoanalytic "scientific" writing, we read:

"Most especially, there is a pull to oral fixation ... Rigid proscriptions around eating and killing animals suggest reaction formation. Oral eroticism is seen in cultural emphasis on generosity, especially around food, institutionalized dependency, totalism etc." (Silvan, 1981, p. 97).

though, perhaps as part of the cultural and political critique of psycho-analysis as it relates to non-Western societies such as India, Bose's person and work have been experiencing a renaissance (Dhar, 2018; Hartnack, 2001; Hiltenbeitel, 2018; Kakar, 1997; Nandy, 1995).

Almost a quarter of a century after the passing away of Bose, there was renewed interest from practicing psychoanalysts in the cultural specificities of psychoanalysis in India as well as its implications for psychoanalytic assumptions and models (Kakar, 1978, 1987b, 1989, 1997; Roland, 1980). To judge from the many papers published by Indian analysts and psychoanalytical therapists in edited books in the last two decades (Akhtar, 2005; Kumar et al., 2018; Vaidyanathan & Kripal, 1999) this interest is burgeoning as the lingering mental colonization is cast off.

In conclusion, I wish to say that as the globalization of ideas picks up pace, psychoanalysis cannot afford to lose the lens through which Indian cultural imagination, as also the imaginations of other major civilizations, have viewed the fundamental questions of human existence, the human mind, and the quest for psychic truth. These cultural imaginations are an invaluable resource for the move away from a universal to a global psychoanalysis that remains aware of but is not limited by its origins in the modern West. I believe that in future, the more important contributions to psychoanalysis, that could rejuvenate its current theoretical/conceptual state, will come from Asia whose ancient and still surviving psycho-philosophical schools have much to contribute. Insights from clinical work embedded in the cultural imaginations of Asian civilizations could spur psychoanalysis to rethink its theories of the human psyche. I hope that this slim volume is a small step in the start of that journey.

CHAPTER 1

Psychoanalysis and cultural imagination: Beginnings of a journey

My own interest in the role of culture in psychoanalysis did not begin as an abstract intellectual exercise but as a matter of vital personal import. Without my quite realizing it at the time, it began with my beginnings as an analyst, some fifty years ago, when I entered a five-day-a-week training analysis with a German analyst at the Sigmund-Freud-Institut in Frankfurt. At first, I registered the role of culture in my analysis as a series of niggling feelings of discomfort whose source remained incomprehensible for many months. Indeed, many years were to pass before I began to comprehend the cultural landscape of the mind in more than a rudimentary fashion and make some sense of my experiences, both as an analysand and as an analyst, in cross-cultural therapeutic dyads (Kakar, 1982, 1987b, 1989, 1997).

I earned very little at the time and in spite of my frequent complaints on my poverty from the couch, I was disappointed when my analyst was prompt in presenting his bill at the end of the month and did not offer to reduce his fees. Without ever asking him directly, I let fall enough hints that he could be helpful in getting me a better-paying job—for instance, as his assistant in the institute where he held an important administrative position.

I did not have any problems in coming to my sessions on time but was resentful that my analyst was equally punctual in ending a session after exactly fifty minutes, sometimes when I had just got going and felt his involvement in my story had been equal to my own. After some months, I realized that my recurrent feelings of estrangement were not due to our cultural differences in forms of politeness, manners of speech, attitudes toward time, or even differences in our aesthetic sensibilities (to me, at that time, Beethoven was just so much noise, while I doubt if he even knew of the existence of Hindustani classical music which so moved me). The estrangement involved much deeper cultural layers of the self, which were an irreducible part of my subjectivity as, I suppose, they were a part of his. In other words, if during a session we sometimes suddenly became strangers to each other, it was because each of us found himself locked into a specific cultural imagination, consisting of a more or less closed system of cultural representations that were not easily accessible to conscious awareness. Glimmers of these deeper cultural layers became visible, although I did not recognize them fully till many years after the analysis ended.

To begin with our specific relationship: in the universe of teacher-healers, I had slotted my analyst into a place normally reserved for a personal guru. It seems that from the beginning of the analysis I had preconsciously envisioned our relationship in terms of a guru–disciple bond, a much more intimate affair than the contractual doctor–patient relationship governing my analyst's professional orientation. In *my* cultural imagination, he was the personification of the wise old sage benevolently directing a sincere and hardworking disciple who had abdicated the responsibility for his own welfare to the guru. My guru model also demanded that my analyst demonstrate his compassion, interest, warmth, and responsiveness much more openly than is usual or even possible in the psychoanalytic model guiding his therapeutic interventions. A handshake with a "Guten Morgen, Herr Kakar" at the beginning of the session and a handshake with a "Auf Wiedersehen, Herr Kakar" at the end of the session, even if accompanied by the beginnings of a smile and a rare twinkle in the eye, were not even starvation rations for someone who had adopted the analyst as his guru. Not that I was uncomfortable with long silences during a session, only that the silence needed to be embedded in other forms of communication. In an earlier essay, I have mentioned that the emphasis on speech and words in analytic communication is counter to the dominant Indian idiom in which words are only a small part of a vast store of signs and semiotics (Kakar, 2018). In psychoanalytic therapy, though, speech reigns supreme. As Freud (1916a) remarked:

> Words were originally magic and to this day words have retained much of their ancient magical power. By words one person can make another blissfully happy or drive him to despair, by words the teacher conveys his knowledge to his pupils, by words the orator carries his audience with him and determines their judgements and decisions. Words provoke affects and are in general the means of mutual influence among men. (p. 17)

Of course, Freud's privileging of words is embedded in a profounder cultural difference in the relationship between speech and truth. Language in the Hindu, and especially in the Buddhist world, is inherently unfit to express what is real. It signifies distance between things and ourselves and thus misleads. Moreover, it inevitably generates illusions and ignorance. To speak is to be drawn into a network of mirages. Truth is unspoken, only silence is true.

In this vision of the relationship between speech and silence, the cultural expectation of the healer-teacher (in the words of the sixteenth-century Indian mystic Dabu) is that:

> The guru speaks first with the mind
> Then with the glance of the eye
> If the disciple fails to understand
> He instructs him at last by word of mouth
> He that understands the spoken word is a common man
> He that interprets the gesture is an initiate
> He that reads the thought of the mind
> Unsearchable, unfathomable, is a god. (Steinmann, 1986, p. 235)

In other words, a Hindu Indian tends to privilege the *presence* of the healer more than his words.

I wonder how many of us realize that the rhythms of our spoken interpretations and silences are not only governed by the course of analysis, by what is happening in the analytic interaction, but are also culturally constituted. That the interpretations of silence, the analyst's of the patient and the patient's of the analyst, also contain cultural signifiers of which both may be unaware.

Our cultural orientations also attached varying importance to different family relationships. For instance, in my childhood, I had spent long periods of my young life in the extended families of my parents. Various uncles, aunts, and cousins had constituted a vital part of my growing up experience. To pay them desultory attention or to reduce them to parental figures in the analytic interpretations felt like a serious impoverishment of my inner world.

This almost exclusive emphasis on the parental couple in psycho-analysis has also to do with the modern Western conception of the family, which has the husband–wife couple as its fulcrum. In the traditional Indian view, which still exerts a powerful influence on how even most modern Indians view marriage, parent–sons and filial bonds among the sons override the significance of the couple as the foundation of the family; the couple is important but secondary. Cultural ideals, then, demand that the universal dream of love that constitutes and seeks to find its culmination in the couple be muted. They enjoin the family to remain vigilant lest the couple becomes a fortress that shuts out all other relationships within the extended family.

On a general level, I realized later, our diverging conceptions of the "true" nature of human relationships were a consequence of a more fundamental divide in our cultural view of the person. In contrast to the modern West, the Indian experience of the self is not that of a bounded, unique individuality. The Indian person is not a self-contained center of awareness interacting with other, similar such individuals. Instead, the traditional Indian, in the dominant image of his culture and in much of his personal experience of the self, is *constituted* of relationships. He is not a monad, but derives his personal nature interpersonally. All affects, needs, and motives are relational and his distresses are disorders of relationships—not only with his human but also with his natural and cosmic orders.

This emphasis on the "dividual" (rather than the individual), transpersonal nature of man (Marriott, 1976) is not limited to traditional, rural India. Even with the urbanized and highly literate persons who form the bulk of patients for psychotherapy, the "relational" orientation is still the "natural" way of viewing the self and the world.

In my own practice later in Delhi, a frequent problem arose when I thought the psychotherapy was going well and the client was well on the road to a modicum of psychological autonomy, and then family members would come to me and complain, "What are you doing to my son/daughter? S/he is becoming independent of us. S/he wants to make her/his own choices now, thinks s/he knows what is best for her/him and doesn't listen to us." I vividly remember the patriarch of a large, extended business family, clad in suit and tie, but with the traditional turban as his headgear, walking into my office one day to discuss the progress in the therapy of his twenty-one-year-old granddaughter who had become clinically depressed as the date for her arranged marriage with the scion of another rich family approached. As her depressive symptoms receded, the girl began to express her opposition to her family's plans for her marriage. Sitting across my desk with both his palms resting on the silver handle of a walking stick, he could barely hide his disappointment in me: "She may be better, doctor, but *we* are much worse!" The families were baffled that the psychoanalytic ideal is to increase the individual's range of choices and not her integration with the family. Transference reactions in a patient may suppress this cultural view during therapy, and even for a while after it has ended, but return as a nagging separation guilt of having abandoned the family.

The yearning for relationships, for the confirming presence of loved persons and the distress aroused by their unavailability or unresponsiveness in time of need, is thus a dominant cultural motif in Indian social relations. The motif is expressed variously but consistently. It is expressed in a person's feelings of helplessness when family members are absent or his difficulty in making decisions alone. In short, Indians tend to characteristically rely on the support of others to go through life and to deal with the exigencies imposed by the outside world (Kakar, 1978).

Could it be that my analyst was like some other Western psychoanalysts who I was reading at the time who would choose to interpret this as a "weakness" in the Indian personality? An evaluation that invariably carries with it the general value implication that independence and initiative are "better" than mutual dependence and community? But it depends, of course, on a culture's vision of a "good society" and "individual merit" whether a person's behavior in relationships is nearer the isolation pole of the fusion–isolation continuum, as postulated by the dominant cultural tradition in the contemporary West, or the fusion pole advocated by traditional Indian culture. To borrow from German philosopher Schopenhauer's imagery, the basic problem of human relationships resembles that of hedgehogs on a cold night. They creep closer to each other for warmth, are pricked by quills and move away, but then get cold again and try to come nearer. This movement to and fro is repeated until an optimum position is reached in which the body temperature is above the freezing point and yet the pain inflicted by the quills (the nearness of the other) is still bearable. Independent of our individual life histories, in the imagination of my Indian culture, in contrast to my analyst's German *Kultur*, the optimum position on this continuum entailed the acceptance of more pain in order to get greater warmth.

The emphasis on connection is also reflected in the Indian image of the body, a core element in the development of the mind. For Ayurveda, one of the chief architects of the Indian image of the human body, the body is intimately connected with nature and the cosmos, and there is nothing in nature without relevance for medicine. The Indian body image, then, stresses an unremitting interchange taking place with the environment, simultaneously accompanied by a ceaseless change within the body. Moreover, in the Indian view, there is no essential difference between body and mind. The body is merely the gross form of matter (*sthulasharira*), just as the mind is a more subtle form of the same matter (*sukshmasharira*); both are different forms of the same body–mind matter—*sharira*.

In contrast, the Western image is of a clearly etched body, sharply differentiated from the rest of the objects in the universe. This vision of the body as a safe stronghold with a limited number of drawbridges that maintain a tenuous contact with the outside world has its own particular cultural consequences. It seems that in Western discourse, both scientific and artistic, there is considerable preoccupation with what is going on *within* the fortress of the individual body. Pre-eminently, one seeks to explain behavior through psychologies that derive from biology, to the relative exclusion of the natural and meta-natural environment. The contemporary search for a genetic basis to all psychological phenomena, irrespective of its scientific merit, is thus a logical consequence of the Western body image. The natural aspects of the environment—the quality of air, the quantity of sunlight, the presence of birds and animals, the plants and the trees—are a priori viewed, when they are considered at all, as irrelevant to intellectual and emotional development. Given the Western image of the body, it is understandable that unconventional Indian beliefs concerning the effects on the *sharira* of planetary constellations, cosmic energies, earth's magnetic fields, seasonal and daily rhythms, and precious stones and metals are summarily consigned to the realm of fantasy, being of interest solely to a "lunatic fringe" of Western society.

It is not only the body but also the emotions that have come to be differently viewed due to the Indian emphasis on connection. As cultural psychologists Richard Shweder and Jonathan Haidt (1993) have pointed out, emotions that have to do with other persons, such as sympathy, feelings of interpersonal communion, and shame, are primary, while the more individualistic emotions, such as anger and guilt, are secondary. If pride is overtly expressed, it is often directed to a collective of which one is a member. Working very hard to win a promotion at work or admission to an elite educational institution is only secondarily connected to the individual need for achievement, which is the primary driving motivation in the West. The first conscious or preconscious thought in the Indian mind is "How happy and proud my family will be!" This is why Indians tend to idealize their families and ancestral background, why there is such prevalence of family myths and of family pride, and why role models for the young are almost exclusively members of the family, very frequently a parent, rather than the movie stars, sporting heroes, or other public figures favored by Western youth.

The greater connective imagination is also congruent with the main thematic content of Indian art. In traditional Indian painting, and especially in temple sculptures, for instance, man is represented not as a discrete presence but as intimately linked to his surroundings, existing in all his myriad connections. These sculptures, as Richard Lannoy has observed, are an "all encompassing labyrinth flux of animal, human and divine … visions of life in the flesh, all jumbled together … suffering and enjoying in a thousand shapes, teeming, devouring, turning into one another" (1971, pp. 76–77). A human being, even the god Krishna, although at the center of an Indian miniature painting, is not central to it. Trees, flowering bushes, cows, peacocks, low hills, other human figures are all important parts of the painting and are connected to the god.

Connective imagination is also the essence of many religious forms. I am especially thinking of Tibetan-Buddhist and Hindu Tantra which have the visualization of the deities and the devotee's union with these mind-created forms as their central spiritual practice. Here, let me mention only one of the many tantric techniques, *nyasa*, in which a Tantric visualizes the goddess and then introjects her into the various parts of his body by touching them. The imaginative world created by the Tantric is not the personal one of the artist (or the psychotic) but is both shared and public in that it is based upon, guided, and formed by the symbolic, iconic network of his religious culture. Another example of religious practice where connective imagination manifests itself is in the daily ritual *puja* of an orthodox Hindu who gets the gods to dwell in the various limbs and parts of his body before he begins to chant his prayers. Indeed, a great attraction of religious practices may well lie in the opportunity they afford the believer to release and exercise his capacity for connective imagination.

Let me add that I am not advancing any simplified dichotomy between my analyst's Western cultural image of an individual, autonomous self and a relational, transpersonal self of my own Hindu culture. Both visions of human experience are present in all the major cultures though a particular culture may, over a length of time, highlight and emphasize one at the expense of the other. What the advent of the Enlightenment in the West has pushed to the background for the last couple of hundred years is still the dominant value of Indian identity, namely that the greatest source of human strength lies in a harmonious integration with the family and the group. This widespread consensus over what I have called the ideology of "familism" asserts that belonging to a community is the fundamental need of man. Only if man truly belongs to such a community, naturally and unselfconsciously, can he enter the river of life and lead a full, creative, and spontaneous life.

In practice, of course—and this is what makes psychoanalytic psycho-therapy in non-Western societies possible—the cultural orientations of patients coming for psychoanalytic therapy are not diametrically opposite to those of the analyst. Most non-Western patients seen by analysts in North America and Europe are "assimilated" to the dominant culture of their host country to varying degrees, the contest between their original and new cultures not yet decisively tilted in favor of the one or the other. Similarly, in non-Western countries, the clients for psychoanalytic therapy—like their analysts—are westernized to varying degrees. In India, for instance, Indian analysts practice in the enclaves of Western modernity in Delhi, Mumbai, Kolkata, and Bengaluru. Here, among the upper and middle classes, there are enough patients, Westernized to various degrees, who are attracted by a Freudian model of man and the causes of his suffering and look toward an analyst as their best ally in the realization of their full individuality.

What could my analyst have done? Did he need to acquire knowledge of my culture and, if so, what kind of knowledge? Would an anthropological, historical, or philosophical grounding in Hindu culture have made him understand me better? Or was it a *psychoanalytical* knowledge of my culture that would have been more helpful? Psychoanalytical knowledge of a culture is not equivalent to its anthropological knowledge although there may be some overlap between the two. Psychoanalytical knowledge is primarily the knowledge of the culture's *imagination*, of its fantasy primarily as encoded in its symbolic products—its myths and folktales, its religious rituals and performances, its popular art, music, literature, and cinema.

Besides asking about the kind of knowledge, we also need to ask the question, "Which culture?" Would a psychoanalytic knowledge of Hindu culture have been sufficient in my case? Yes, I am a Hindu but also a Punjabi Khatri by birth. That is, my overarching Hindu culture has been mediated by my strong regional culture as a Punjabi and further by my Khatri caste. This Hindu Punjabi Khatri culture has been further modified by an agnostic father and a more traditional, believing mother, both of whom were also westernized to varying degrees. Is it not too much to expect any analyst to acquire this kind of prior cultural knowledge about his patients? On the other hand, is it OK for the analyst not to have *any* knowledge of his patient's cultural imagination? Or does the truth, as it often does, lie somewhere in the middle?

But now comes the surprise. My analyst was very good—sensitive, insightful, patient. And I discovered that as my analysis progressed, my feelings of estrangement that had given rise to all these questions became fewer and fewer. What was happening? Was the cultural part of my self becoming less salient as the analysis touched ever-deeper layers of the self, as many psychoanalysts have claimed?

Most analysts have followed George Devereux's (1953) lead in maintaining that all those who seek help from a psychoanalyst have in common many fundamental and universal components in their personality structure. Together with the universality of the psychoanalytic method, these common factors sufficiently equip the analyst to understand and help his patient, irrespective of the patient's cultural background, a view reiterated by a panel of the American Psychoanalytic Association on the role of culture in psychoanalysis more than fifty-five years ago (Jackson, 1968). There are certainly difficulties such as the ones enumerated by Ticho (1971) in treating patients of a different culture: a temporary impairment of the analyst's technical skills, empathy for the patient, diagnostic acumen, the stability of self and object representations, and the stirring up of countertransference manifestations which may not be easily distinguishable from stereotypical reactions to the foreign culture. Generally, though, given the analyst's empathetic stance and the rules of analytic procedure, these difficulties are temporary and do not require a change in analytic technique. It is useful but not essential for the analyst to understand the patient's cultural heritage.

I believe that these conclusions on the role of culture in psychoanalytic therapy, which would seem to apply to my own experience, are superficially true but deeply mistaken. For what I did, and I believe most patients do, was to enthusiastically, if unconsciously, acculturate to the analyst's culture—in my case, both to his broader Western, north European culture and to his particular Freudian psychoanalytic culture. The latter, we know, is informed by a vision of human experience that emphasizes man's individuality and his self-contained psyche. In the psychoanalytic vision, in Kenneth Kenniston's words (Adams, 1976), each of us lives in his own subjective world, pursuing pleasures and private fantasies, constructing a life and a fate which will vanish when our time is over. It emphasizes the desirability of reflective awareness of one's inner states, insistence that our psyches harbor deeper secrets than we care to confess, the existence of an objective reality that can be known, and an essential complexity and tragedy of life where many wishes are fated to remain unfulfilled.

Now, we know that every form of therapy is also an enculturation. As Fancher (1993) remarks:

> By the questions we ask, the things we empathize with, the themes we pick for our comment, the ways we conduct ourselves toward the patient, the language we use—by all these and a host of other ways, we communicate to the patient our notions (Freudian, Jungian, Kleinian, Lacanian etc.) of what is "normal" and normative. Our interpretations (Freudian, Jungian, Kleinian, Lacanian etc.) of the origins of a patient's issues reveal in pure form our assumptions of what causes what, what is problematic about life, where the patient did not get what s/he needed, what should have been otherwise. (pp. 89–90)

As a patient in the throes of transference love, I was exquisitely attuned to the cues to my analyst's values, beliefs, and vision of the fulfilled life, which even the most non-intrusive of analysts cannot help but scatter during the therapeutic process. I was quick to pick up the cues that unconsciously shaped my reactions and responses accordingly, with their overriding goal to please and be pleasing in the eyes of the beloved analyst. My intense need to be "understood" by the analyst, a need I shared with every patient, gave birth to an unconscious force that made me underplay those cultural parts of my self which I believed would be too foreign to the analyst's experience. In the transference-love, what I sought was closeness to the analyst, including the sharing of his culturally shaped interests, attitudes, and beliefs. This intense need to be close and to be understood, paradoxically by removing parts of the self from the analytic arena of understanding, was epitomized by the fact that I soon started dreaming in German, the language of my analyst, something I have not done before or after my analysis.

This tendency to excise a cultural part of the self is accelerated when the analysis is conducted in a language other than the mother tongue wherein much of one's native culture is encoded. One's mother tongue, the language of one's childhood, is intimately linked with emotionally colored sensory-motor experiences. Psychoanalysis in a language that is not the patient's own is often in danger of leading to "operational thinking," that is, verbal expressions lacking associational links with feelings, symbols, and memories (Basch-Kahre, 1984). However grammatically correct and rich in its vocabulary, the alien language suffers from emotional poverty, certainly as far as early memories are concerned.

The emotional poverty of language that is acquired much later has been dramatically demonstrated by an experiment in which subjects are asked the following question. A train is approaching at high speed. If you can push one individual on the track, stopping the train, it will save the lives of six others standing a little distance down the track. Will you push that individual in front of the train? Asked and answered in the mother tongue, most people show signs of an emotional dilemma and would not push the person to his death. The same question in the acquired language evokes much greater calculated rationality and the readiness to push one person in order to save the lives of six.

How should a psychoanalyst, then, approach the issue of cultural difference of his client in his practice? The ideal situation would be that this difference exists only minimally, in the sense that the analyst has obtained a psychoanalytic knowledge of the patient's culture through a long immersion in its daily life and its myths, its folklore and literature, its language and its music—an absorption not through the bones as in the case of his patient, but through the head—and the heart. Anything less than this maximalist position has the danger of the analyst succumbing to the lure of cultural stereotyping in dealing with the particularities of the patient's experience. In cross-cultural therapeutic dyads, little knowledge is indeed a dangerous thing, collapsing important differences, assuming sameness when only similarities exist. What the analyst needs is not a detailed knowledge of the patient's culture but a serious questioning and awareness of the assumptions underlying his own, that is, the culture he was born into and the culture in which he has been professionally socialized as a psychoanalyst.

In other words, what I am suggesting is that in the absence of the possibility of obtaining a deep knowledge of his patient's cultural imagination, the analyst needs to strive for a state of affairs where the patient's feelings of estrangement because of his cultural differences from the analyst are minimized and the patient does not cut off, or only minimally cuts off the cultural part of the self from the therapeutic situation. This is possible only if the analyst can convey a cultural openness which comes from becoming aware of his own culture's fundamental propositions about human nature, human experience, the fulfilled human life, and then to acknowledge their relativity by seeing them as cultural products, embedded in a particular place and time. He needs to become sensitive to the hidden existence of what Kohut (1979, p. 12) called "health and maturity moralities" of his particular analytical school. He needs to root out cultural judgments about what constitutes psychological maturity, gender-appropriate behaviors, "positive" or "negative" resolutions of developmental conflicts and complexes, that often appear in the garb of universally valid truths.

Given that ethnocentrism, the tendency to view alien cultures in terms of our own, and unresolved cultural chauvinism, are the patrimony of all human beings, including that of psychoanalysts, the acquisition of cultural openness is not an easy task. Cultural biases can lurk in the most unlikely places. For instance, to judge from the number of articles in psychoanalytic journals and books, psychoanalysis has traditionally accorded a high place to artistic creativity. To paint, sculpt, engage in literary and musical pursuits have not always and everywhere enjoyed the high prestige they do in modern Western societies. In other historical periods, many civilizations, including mine to this day, placed religious creativity at the top of their scale of desirable human endeavors. Psychoanalysts need to imagine, without condescension, that in such cultural settings, the following conclusion to a case report could be an example of a successful therapeutic outcome: "The patient's visions increased markedly in quantity and quality and the devotional mood took hold of her for longer and longer periods of time."

I would suggest that for optimal psychotherapy with patients from different cultures, what a psychoanalytical therapist needs is not an exhaustive knowledge of the patient's culture but a reflective openness to and interrogation of his own cultural origins. A therapist can evaluate his progress toward this openness by the increase in his feelings of curiosity and wonder in his countertransference when the cultural parts of the patient's self find their voice in therapy, when the temptation to pathologize the cultural part of his patient's beliefs and behavior decreases, when his own values no longer appear as normal and virtuous, and when his wish to instruct the patient in these values diminishes markedly.

The journey (continued)

Many of my first patients when I returned to India in 1975 and set up a practice in Delhi were traditional Indians who had made the rounds of exorcists, Ayurvedic and Unani medical practitioners, and other traditional healers of mental suffering. Unlike most Western patients seeking psychotherapy, they came to me without any knowledge of psychoanalysis but in hope of help from a "brain doctor" who was cloaked in the (false) prestige of modern Western medicine. I have described my failures and what I learnt from these at another place (Kakar, 1982) and will illustrate an invaluable lesson from one of the cases.

Case study 1

Ramnath was a fifty-one-year-old man who owned a grocery shop in the oldest part of the city of Delhi. When he came to see me, he was suffering from a number of complaints, though he desired my help for only one of them—an unspecified "fearfulness." This anxiety, of less than three years' duration, was a relatively new development. His migraine headaches, on the other hand, went back to his adolescence. Ramnath attributed them to an excess of "wind" in the stomach, which periodically rose up and pressed against the veins in his head. He has always had a nervous stomach. It has never been quite as bad as it was in the months following his marriage some thirty years ago, when he suffered from severe stomach cramps and an alarming weight loss. He was first taken to the hospital by his father, where he was x-rayed and tested. Finding nothing wrong with him, the doctors had prescribed a variety of vitamins and tonics which were not of much help. Older family members and friends had then recommended a nearby ojha—"sorcerer" is too fierce a translation for this mild-mannered professional of ritual exorcism—who diagnosed his condition as being the result of magic practiced by an enemy, namely his newly acquired father-in-law. The rituals to counteract the enemy magic were expensive, as was the yellowish liquid emetic prescribed by the ojha, which periodically forced Ramnath to empty his stomach with gasping heaves. In any event, he was fully cured within two months of the ojha's treatment, and the cramps and weight loss have not recurred.

Before coming to see me about his "fearfulness," Ramnath had been treated with drugs by various doctors: by allopaths (as Western-style doctors are called in India) as well as homeopaths, by the vaids of Hindu medicine as well as the hakims of Islamic medical tradition. He had consulted psychiatrists, ingested psychotropic drugs, and submitted to therapy. He had gone through the rituals of two ojhas and was thinking of consulting a third who had been highly recommended.

His only relief came through the weekly gathering of the local chapter of the Brahmakumari (literally "Virgins of Brahma") sect which he had recently joined. The communal meditations and singing gave him a feeling of temporary peace, and his nights were no longer so restless. Ramnath was puzzled by the persistence of his anxious state and its various symptoms. He had tried to be a good man, he said, according to his dharma, which is both the "right conduct" of his caste and the limits imposed by his own character and predispositions. He had worshipped the gods and attended services in the temple with regularity, even contributing generously toward the consecration of a Krishna idol in his native village in Rajasthan. He did not have any bad habits, he asserted. Tea and cigarettes, yes, but for a couple of years he had abjured even these minor though pleasurable addictions. Yet the anxiety persisted, unremitting and unrelenting.

Since it is culture rather than psyche which is the focus of this case, let me essay a cultural analysis rather than a psycho-analysis of Ramnath's condition. At first glance, Ramnath's cognitive space in matters of illness and well-being seems incredibly cluttered. Gods and spirits, community and family, food and drink, personal habits and character, all seem to be somehow intimately involved in the maintenance of health. Yet these and other factors such as biological infection, social pollution, and cosmic displeasure—all of which most Hindus would also acknowledge as causes of ill health—only point to the recognition of a person's simultaneous existence in different orders of being; of the person being a body, a psyche, and a social being at the same time. Ramnath's experience of his illness may appear alien to Europeans only because, as I have elaborated elsewhere (Kakar, 1982), the body, the psyche, and the community do not possess fixed, immutable meanings across the cultures.

As I have mentioned above, the concept of the body and the understanding of its processes are not quite the same in India as they are in the West. The Hindu body, portrayed in relevant cultural texts predominantly in imagery from the vegetable kingdom, is much more intimately connected with the cosmos than the clearly etched Western body, which is sharply differentiated from the rest of the objects in the universe.

The psyche—the Hindu "subtle body"—is not primarily a psychological category in India. It is closer to the ancient Greek meaning of the "psyche," the source of all vital activities and psychic processes, and considered capable of persisting in its disembodied state after death. Similarly, for many Indians, the community consists not only of living members of the family and the social group but also of ancestral and other spirits as well as the gods and goddesses who populate the Hindu cosmos. An Indian is inclined to believe that his or her illness can reflect a disturbance in any one of these orders of being, while the symptoms may also be manifested in the other orders. If a treatment, say, in the bodily order fails, one is quite prepared to reassign the cause of the illness to a different order and undergo its particular curing regimen—prayers or exorcisms, for instance—without losing regard for other methods of treatment.

The involvement of all orders of being in health and illness means that an Indian is generally inclined to seek more than one cause for illness in especially intractable cases. An Indian tends to view these causes as complementary rather than exclusive and arranges them in a hierarchical order by identifying an immediate cause as well as others that are more remote. The causes are arranged in concentric circles, with the outer circle including all the inner ones.

To continue with our case study example:

> Ramnath had suffered migraine headaches since his adolescence. Doctors of traditional Hindu medicine, Ayurveda, had diagnosed the cause as a humoral disequilibrium—an excess of "wind" in the stomach which periodically rose up and pressed against the veins in his head—and prescribed Ayurvedic drugs, dietary restrictions, as well as liberal doses of aspirin. Such a disequilibrium is usually felt to be compounded by bad habits which, in turn, demand changes in personal conduct. When an illness like Ramnath's persists, its stubborn intensity will be linked with his unfavorable astrological conditions, requiring palliative measures such as a round of prayers (puja).

The astrological "fault" probably will be further traced back to the bad karma of a previous birth about which, finally, nothing can be done—except, perhaps, the cultivation of a stoic endurance with the help of the weekly meetings of the Virgins of Brahma sect.

I saw Ramnath three times a week in psychoanalytic therapy for twenty-one sessions before he decided to terminate the treatment. At the time, although acutely aware of my deficiencies as a novice, I had placed the blame for the failure of the therapy on the patient or, to be more exact, on the cultural factors involved in his decision. Some of these were obvious. Ramnath had slotted me into a place normally reserved for a personal guru. From the beginning, he envisioned not a contractual doctor–patient relationship but a much more intimate guru–disciple bond that would allow him to abdicate responsibility for his life. He was increasingly dismayed that I as a psychoanalyst did not dispense wise counsel but expected the client to talk, and that I wanted to follow his lead rather than impose my own views or directions on the course of our sessions. I did not know then that Ramnath's "guru fantasy," namely the existence of someone, somewhere—now discovered in my person—who will heal the wounds suffered in all past relationships and remove the blights on the soul so that it shines anew in its pristine state, was not inherent in his Indianness but common across many cultures. Irrespective of their conscious subscription to the ideology of egalitarianism and a more contractual doctor–patient relationship, my European and American patients, too, approached analysis and the analyst with a full-blown "guru fantasy" which, however, was more hidden and less accessible to consciousness than in the case of Ramnath. I will return to the "guru fantasy" later.

Rather than Ramnath's expectations, I now realize, it was my disappointment which caused the therapy to flounder: I had expected Ramnath to be an individual in the sense of someone whose consciousness had been molded in a crucible which is commonly regarded as having come into existence as part of the psychological revolution in the wake of the Enlightenment in Europe. This revolution, of course, is supposed to have narrowed the older, metaphysical scope of the mind as an isolated island of individual consciousness, profoundly aware of its almost limitless subjectivity and its infantile tendency to heedless projection and illusion. Psychoanalysis, I believed, with some justification, is possible only with a person who is individual in this special sense.

If most psychoanalytic case histories, whether in Western or non-Western worlds, analysands, except for their different neurotic or character disturbances, sound pretty much like each other (and like their analysts), then this is because they all share the post-Enlightenment worldview of what constitutes an individual. In a fundamental sense, psychoanalysis does not have a cross-cultural context but takes place in the same context across different societies; it works in the established (and expanding) enclaves of psychological modernity around the world. We can therefore better understand why psychoanalysis in India began in Calcutta—the first capital of the British Empire in India where Indians began their engagement and confrontation with post-Enlightenment Western thought—before extending itself and, till recently, virtually limiting itself to Mumbai, which prides itself on its cosmopolitan character and cultural "modernity." It is also comprehensible that the clientele for psychoanalysis in India consists overwhelmingly—though not wholly—of individuals (and their family members) who are involved in modern professions like journalism, advertising, academia, law, medicine, and so on. In the sociological profile, at least, this clientele does not significantly differ from one which seeks psychoanalytic therapy in Europe and America.

Ramnath, I believed, was not an individual in the sense that he lacked "psychological modernity." He had manfully tried to understand the psychoanalytic model of inner conflict rooted in life history that was implied in my occasional interventions. It seemed clear to me that this went against his cultural model of psychic distress and healing wherein the causes for his suffering lay outside himself and had little to do with his biography—black magic by father-in-law, disturbed planetary constellations, bad karma from previous life, disturbed humoral equilibrium. He was thus not suitable for psychoanalytic therapy, and perhaps I had given up on him before he gave up on me. But Ramnath, I realized later, like many of my other traditional Hindu patients, had an individuality which is embedded in and expressed in terms from the Hindu cultural universe. This individuality is accessible to psycho-analysis if the therapist is willing and able to build the required bridges from a modern to a traditional individuality. The Indian analyst has to be prepared, for instance, to interpret the current problems of such a patient in terms of his or her bad karma—feelings, thoughts, and actions—not from a previous existence but from a forgotten life, the period of infancy and childhood, his or her "prehistory." Let me elaborate on this distinction between traditional and modern individuals who both share what I believe is the essence of psychological modernity.

Psychological modernity, although strongly associated with the post-Enlightenment, is nevertheless not identical with it. The core of psychological modernity is internalization rather than externalization. I use internalization here as a sensing by the person of a psyche in the Greek sense, an animation from within rather than without. Experientially, this internalization is a recognition that one is possessed of a mind in all its complexity. It is the acknowledgment, however vague, unwilling, or conflicted, of a subjectivity that destines one to episodic suffering through some of one's ideas and feelings. In psychoanalysis, these could be described as murderous rage, envy, and possessive desire seeking to destroy and to keep alive those one loves. Simultaneously comes the knowledge, at some level of awareness, that the mind can help in containing and processing disturbed thoughts, as can the family and the group (Bollas, 1992). In Hindu terms, it is a person's sense and acknowledgment of the primacy of the "subtle body"—the *sukshmasharira*—in human action and of human suffering as caused by the workings of the five passions: sexual desire, rage, greed, infatuation, and egotism.

Similarly, Buddhists, too, describe human suffering as being due to causes internal to the individual: cognitive factors such as a perceptual cloudiness causing misperception of external objects but also affective causes such as agitation and worry—the elements of anxiety, greed, and envy—which form the cluster of grasping attachment. This internalization is the essence of "individuation" and of psychological modernity, which has always been a part of what Hindus call the "more evolved" beings in traditional civilizations. The fact that this core of individuation is expressed in a religious rather than a psychological idiom should not prevent us from recognizing its importance as an ideal of maturity in traditional civilizations such as Hindu India. The "evolved" Hindu in the past or even in the present, who has little to do with the post-Enlightenment West, thus interprets the epic *Mahabharata* as an account of inner conflict in man's soul rather than of outer hostilities among the Pandavas and Kauravas.

The "evolved beings" in India, including the most respected gurus, have always held that the guru, too, is only seemingly a person but is actually a function, a transitional object in modern parlance, as are all the various gods who are also only aspects of the self. "The guru is the disciple, but perfected, complete," says Muktananda (1983). "When he forms a relationship with the guru, the disciple is in fact forming a relationship with his own best self" (p. ix). At the end of your sadhana, burn the guru, say the Tantrics; kill the Buddha if you meet him on the way, is a familiar piece of Zen Buddhist wisdom. All of them, gurus or gods (as also the analyst), have served the purpose of internalization—a specific mode of relating to and experiencing the self—and are dispensable.

Psychological modernity is thus not coterminous with historical modernity; nor are its origins in a specific geographical location, even if it received a sharp impetus from the European Enlightenment. My biggest error in Ramnath's case was in making a sharp dichotomy between a "Hindu" cultural view of the interpersonal and transpersonal nature of the person and a modern "Western" view of the person's individual and instinctual nature, and assuming that since Ramnath was not an individual in the latter sense, he was not an individual at all.

Cultural imagination

The continuing resistance in psychoanalysis to acknowledge the crucial role of culture in the constitution of the psyche is not due to any obdurate refusal by contemporary analysts to question the essentialist "psychic unity of mankind" view underlying Freud's grand meta-psychological constructions. It is more due to the self-understanding of psychoanalysis as a unique, "depth" psychology, in contrast to the more "superficial" psychologies that are oriented toward the cultural and social surrounds of the person. Psychoanalysis considers itself unique in that it can access the instinctual forces operating in the depth of the human psyche, in the unconscious; these are forces of man's biological nature that precede culture. But what if this bedrock of psychoanalytic thought is susceptible to doubt? As Mitchell and

Harris (2004) observe, it has become increasingly apparent how culturally specific and socially constructed our ideas of nature actually are. They give the example of American psychoanalysis, influenced by the idea of nature as friendly and collaborative, in contrast to central European ideas of nature as dark and dangerous (e.g., the primeval German forest). Whereas in Freud's vision the unconscious forces of nature (id) clash with human culture, "the American psychoanalytic vision portrays nature (and biology) as less inherently conflictual with human concerns, but instead as overlapping and interpenetrating them" (Mitchell & Harris, 2004, p. 180).

For the Indian idea of nature and thus also of human nature and the unconscious, let me turn to the "origin myth"[4] of the philosopher-poet Rabindranath Tagore. In a letter to his friend C. F. Andrews, Tagore writes (n.d.):[5]

> From the beginning of their history the Western races have had to deal with nature as their antagonist. This fact has emphasized in their mind the dualistic aspect of truth, the eternal conflict between good and evil. Thus the West has kept up the spirit of fight in the heart of their civilization. They seek victory and cultivate power.

The environment in which the Aryan immigrants found themselves in India was that of the forest. The forest, unlike the desert or rock or sea, is living; it gives shelter and nourishment to life. In such a surrounding the ancient forest dwellers of India realized the spirit of harmony with the universe, and emphasized in their mind the monistic aspect of truth. They sought the realization of their soul through the union with all.

The forest in the Indian cultural imagination is a place of calm and peace, free of the turbulence of urban life. In the Hindu view of the life cycle, vanaprastha, "retreat to the forest," is the stage of life where the older person is enjoined to detach themselves from the life of the "householder" and retreat to a forest hermitage to contemplate wider social and existential concerns.

---

[4] Like Freud's (1921c) Ur myth of the primal horde, Tagore's origin myth of Aryans' encounter with the forest environment in India is a "Just-So Story," as Freud calls it, that although conjectural, may "bring coherence and understanding into more and more new regions" (p. 122).

[5] Probably first week of April, 1921.

The Indian vision of nature and of an unconscious id is thus of an essentially benign entity that nourishes human concerns and is indispensable in realizing the purpose of human life. The Indian idea of the unconscious coincides with the unconscious chitta of Yoga philosophy, an unconscious that is bound to the body at birth.

Chitta is visualized as a lake, swirling with eddies of desire and attachment. These eddies (not the Kleinian devastating storms) are sought to be stilled by the practice of Yoga that returns the chitta to its natural state where the ultimate aim of human life can be realized. Psychoanalysts would have difficulty in accepting the "mystical" goal of Yoga as relevant for their own discipline. The focus of yogic practice, the calming of chitta, *chitta vritti nirodha*, however, will be familiar to analysts from Freud's aphorism on the analytic cure, "Where id was, there shall ego be" (Freud, 1933a, p. 80), even if this formulation is now held by most practitioners to be an oversimplification of the analytic process.

Indian psychoanalysis, then, will not only subscribe to the unconscious as a repository of repressions and deprivations but also conceive it as a fount of the healing Eros. Eros, like desire, is a concept difficult to pin down with sexuality at one pole of its continuum and the life preservation instinct or life energy at the other, with many shades of desire and love along the way. It is the life giving and life sustaining force that is the source of an intense feeling of being alive, of spontaneity, creativity, and especially *connectivity* to both our human and nonhuman environment. When Freud writes that the power of the id expresses the true purpose of the individual organism's life and this consists in the satisfaction of its innate needs, then the flow of Eros is an innate need of the unconscious. An Indian psychoanalysis will visualize the analytic process as removing the blockages and inhibitions, accumulated over the life cycle and especially during early childhood, to the flow of Eros in mind, body, and soul.

Another Indian psycho-philosophical school, Tantra, shares a similar imagery, namely the release and flow of kundalini through the blocked chakras of the mind–body entity. In so far as the focus of much of contemporary psychoanalysis is on attenuating psychic pain—fear, guilt, anxiety, depression, the sustained engagement with loss and mourning— we sometimes tend to forget that the feeling of aliveness in the full flow of Eros is the destination (if not always reached) of the analytic journey after the many sites of psychic pain have been negotiated.

In conclusion

During the journey, then, it became important to constantly remain aware of the Indian cultural imagination in my clinical work and writings but without sinking into traditionalism and becoming the apologist of tradition. On the other hand, because of the presence of many Western cultural assumptions in psychoanalysis, as indeed there are in most social sciences, I also needed to critically look at psycho-analytic concepts without junking a discipline which has considerable explanatory power, not to speak of its individual and social emanci-patory potential. Even as I question much of psychoanalytic super-structure, I continue to stand on its foundations and subscribe to its basic assumptions: the importance of the unconscious part of the mind in our thought and actions, the vital significance of early childhood experiences for later life, the importance of Eros in human motivation, and the dynamic interplay, including conflict, between the conscious and unconscious parts of the mind. All the rest is up for grabs and just as we have begun to talk of modernity in the plural, of different modernities, perhaps we will soon be talking of Japanese, Chinese, Korean, Iranian, and Indian psychoanalyses.

My own journey, the project of "translation" in the last fifty years of work with Indian and Western patients, has thus been guided by the understanding that the translation of psychoanalysis in a non-Western culture must give equal value to both the languages, of psychoanalysis and of the cultural imagination in which psychoanalysis is being received.

CHAPTER 2

Maternal enthrallment: The pre-eminence of the maternal-feminine in Hindu India

On April 11, 1929, Girindrasekhar Bose, the founder and first president of the Indian Psychoanalytical Society, wrote to Freud on the difference he had observed in the psychoanalytic treatment of Indian and Western patients:

> Of course I do not expect that you would accept offhand my reading of the Oedipus situation. I do not deny the importance of the castration threat in European cases; my argument is that the threat owes its efficiency to its connection with the wish to be female [Freud in a previous letter had gently chided Bose with understating the efficiency of the castration threat]. The real struggle lies between the desire to be a male and its opposite, the desire to be a female. I have already referred to the fact that castration threat is very common in Indian society but my Indian patients do not exhibit castration symptoms to such a marked degree as my European cases. The desire to be female is more easily unearthed in Indian male patients than in European … The Oedipus mother is very often a combined parental image and this is a fact of great importance. I have reason to believe that much of the motivation of the "maternal deity" is traceable to this source.

Freud's reply is courteous and diplomatic: "I am fully impressed by the difference in the castration reaction between Indian and European patients and promise to keep my attention fixed on the opposite wish you accentuate. The latter is too important for a hasty decision" (Sinha, 1966, p. 66).

In another paper, Bose (1950) elaborates on his observations and explains them through his theory of opposite wishes:

> During my analysis of Indian patients I have never come across a case of castration complex in the form in which it has been described by European observers. This fact would seem to indicate that the castration idea develops as a result of environmental conditions acting on some more primitive trend in the subject. The difference in social environment of Indians and Europeans is responsible for the difference in modes of expression in two cases. It has been usually proposed that threat of castration in early childhood days, owing to some misdemeanour, is directly responsible for the complex, but histories of Indian patients seem to disprove this. (p. 74)

Bose then goes on to say that though the castration threat is extremely common—in girls it takes the form of chastisement by snakes—the difference in Indian reactions to it is due to children growing up naked till the ages of nine to ten years (girls till seven) so that the difference between the sexes never comes as a surprise. The castration idea which comes up symbolically in dreams as decapitation, a cut on a finger, or a sore in some parts of the body has behind it the "primitive" idea of being a woman.

Indeed, reading early Indian case histories, one is struck by the fluidity of the patients' cross-sexual and generational identifications. In the Indian patient the fantasy of taking on the sexual attributes of both the parents seems to have relatively easier access to awareness. Bose, for instance, in one of his vignettes (Bose, 1948) tells us of a middle-aged lawyer who, with reference to his parents, sometimes took up an active male sexual role, treating both of them as females in his unconscious, and sometimes a female attitude, especially toward the father, craving for a child from him. In the male role, sometimes he identified himself with his father and felt a sexual craving for the mother; on the other occasions his unconscious mind built up a composite of both the parents toward which male sexual needs were directed; it is in this attitude that he made his father give birth to a child like a woman in his dream (p. 158).

Another young Bengali (Bose, 1949), whenever he thought of a particular man, felt with a hallucinatory intensity that his penis and testes vanished altogether and were replaced by female genitalia. While defecating he felt he heard the peremptory voice of his guru asking, "Have you given me a child yet?" In many of his dreams, he was a man, whereas his father and brothers had become women. During intercourse with his wife he tied a handkerchief over his eyes as it gave him the feeling of being a veiled bride while he fantasized his own penis as that of his father and his wife's vagina as that of his mother.

In my own work that began fifty years after Bose's contributions of which I was only vaguely aware, I was struck by the comparable patterns in Indian mental life we observed independently of each other, and this in spite of our different emotional predilections, analytic styles, theoretical preoccupations, geographical locations, and historical situations. Such a convergence further strengthens my belief, shared by every practicing analyst, that there is no absolute arbitrariness in our representation of the inner world. There is unquestionably something that resists, a something which can only be characterized by the attribute "psychical reality" which both the analyst and the analysand help discover and give meaning to.

Judged by its frequency of occurrence in clinical work and its pre-eminence in the Hindu cultural imagination, the theme of what I call "maternal enthrallment" appears to be the hegemonic (to use the fashionable Gramscian term) narrative of the Hindu family drama (Kakar, 1989). The reason why I mention cultural imagination in conjunction with clinical work, when advancing a generalized psychoanalytic proposition about the Indian cultural context, is simple. Clinical psychoanalysis is generally limited to a small sample from three or four large Indian metropolises. It cannot adequately take into account the heterogeneity of a country of over a billion people with its regional, linguistic, religious, and caste divisions. Clinical cases can, at best, generate hypotheses about cultural particularities. The further testing of these hypotheses is done (and remains true to psychoanalytic intention and enterprise) by testing them in the crucible of the culture's imagination before psychoanalytic propositions about the culture can be advanced.

Maternal enthrallment consists of the wish to get away from the mother together with the dread of separation, the wish to destroy the engulfing mother who also ensures the child's survival, and, especially in the male child, incestuous desire coexisting with the terror inspired by an overwhelming female sexuality. Maternal enthrallment is the largely unconscious underside of the overt and ubiquitous idealization of the mother, especially by the Hindu son, which will influence his later relationships and unconscious attitudes toward women. Maternal enthrallment is not peculiarly Indian but to a lesser or greater degree a universal part of the psyche. Yet it is undeniable that its psychic import in the formation of subjectivity also has compelling cultural components, such as an Indian infant's prolonged contact with the mother's breast and body described in the Introduction.

In the Indian context, I would suggest, maternal enthrallment is the dominant narrative of male psychological development, in contrast, say, to the father–son conflicts around generational ascendancy that was long emphasized in Western psychoanalytic writings. My main argument is that the hegemonic narrative of Hindu Indian culture as far as male development is concerned is neither that of Freud's Oedipus nor that of Christianity's Adam. One of the more dominant narratives of this culture is that of Devi, the great goddess, especially in her manifold expressions as mother in the inner world of the Hindu son. In India at least, a primary task of psychoanalysis, the science of imagination or even "the science of illusion"—Mayalogy—is to grapple with Mahamaya—"The Great Illusion," as the goddess is also called. Of course, it is not my intention to deny or underestimate the importance of the powerful mother in Western psychoanalysis. All I seek to suggest is that certain forms of the maternal-feminine are more central in Indian myths and psyche than in their Western counterparts. I would then like to begin my exposition with the first ten minutes of an analytic session.

Case study 2

The patient is a twenty-six-year-old social worker who has been in analysis for three years. He comes four times a week with each session lasting fifty minutes and conducted in the classical manner with the patient lying on the couch and the analyst sitting in a chair behind him. He entered analysis not because of any pressing personal problems but because he thought it would help him professionally. In this particular session, he begins with a fantasy he had while he was on a bus. The fantasy was of a tribe living in the jungle which unclothes its dead and hangs them on the trees. M, the patient, visualized a beautiful woman hanging on one of the trees. He imagined himself coming at night and having intercourse with the woman. Other members of the tribe are eating parts of the hanging corpses. The fantasy is immediately followed by the recollection of an incident from the previous evening. M was visiting his parents' home where he had lived till recently when he married and set up his own household. This step was not only personally painful but also unusual for his social milieu where sons normally brought their wives to live in their parental home. His younger sister, with her three-year-old son, was also visiting at the same time. M felt irritated by the anxious attention his mother and grandmother gave the boy. The grandmother kept on telling the child not to go and play out of the house, to be careful of venturing too far, and so on. On my remarking that perhaps he recognized himself in the nephew, M exclaimed with rare resentment, "Yes, all the women [his mother, grandmother, his father's brother's wife, and his father's unmarried sister who lived with them] were always doing the same with me."

Beginning with these ten minutes of a session, I would like to unroll M's conflicts around maternal representations and weave them together with the central maternal configurations of Indian cultural imagination. Because of this particular objective, my presentation of further material from M's analysis is bound to be subject to what Donald Spence (1986) has called "narrative smoothing." A case history, though it purports to be a story that is true, is actually always at the intersection of fact and fable. Its fictional quality, though, arises less from the commissions in imagination than from omissions in reality.

Born in a lower middle-class family in a large village near Delhi, M is the eldest of three brothers and two sisters. His memories of growing up, till well into youth, are pervaded by the maternal phalanx of the four women. Like his mother, who in his earliest memories stands out as a distinct figure from a maternal-feminine continuum to be then reabsorbed into it, M, too, often emerges from and retreats into femininity. In the transference, the fantasies of being a woman are not especially disturbing; neither are the fantasies of being an infant suckling at a breast which he has grown onto my exaggeratedly hairy chest. One of his earliest recollections is of a woman who used to pull at the penises of the little boys playing out in the street. M never felt afraid when the woman grabbed at his own penis. In fact, he rather liked it, reassured that he had a penis at all or at least enough of one for the woman to acknowledge its existence.

Bathed, dressed, combed, and caressed by one or the other of the women, M's wishes and needs were met before they were even articulated. Food, especially the milk-based Indian sweets, was constantly pressed on him. Even now, on his visits to the family, the first question by one of the women pertains to what he would like to eat. For a long time during the analysis, whenever a particular session was stressful because of what he considered a lack of maternal empathy in my interventions, M felt compelled to go to a restaurant in town where he would first gorge himself on sweets before he returned home.

Besides the omnipresence of women, my most striking impressions of M's early memories is their diurnal location in night and their primarily tactile quality. Partly, this has to do with the crowded, public living arrangements of the Indian family. Here, even the notions of privacy are absent, not to speak of such luxuries as separate bedrooms for parents and children. Sleeping in the heat with little or no clothes next to one of his caretakers, an arm or a leg thrown across the maternal body, there is one disturbing memory which stands out clearly. This is of M's penis erect against the buttocks of his sleeping mother and his reluctance to move away, struggling against the feelings of shame and embarrassment that she may wake up and notice the forbidden touch. Later, in adolescence, the mothers are replaced by visiting cousins sharing mattresses spread out in the room or on the roof, furtive rubbings of bodies and occasional genital contact while other members of the extended family are in various stages of sleep.

Embedded in this blissful abundance of maternal flesh and promiscuity of touch, however, is a nightmare. Ever since childhood and persisting well into the initial phases of the analysis, M would often scream in his sleep while a vague, dark shape threatened to envelop him. At these times only his father's awakening him with the reassurance that everything was all right helped M compose himself for renewed slumber. The father, a gentle, retiring man who left early in the morning for work and returned home late at night, was otherwise a dim figure hovering at the outskirts of an animated family life.

In the very first sessions of the analysis, M talked of a sexual compulsion which he found embarrassing to acknowledge. The compulsion consisted of travelling in a crowded bus and seeking to press close to the hips of any plump, middle-aged woman standing in the aisle. It was vital for his ensuing excitement that the woman have her back to him. If she ever turned to face M, with the knowledge of his desire in her eyes, his erection immediately subsided and he would hurriedly move away with intense feelings of shame. After marriage, too, the edge of his desire was often at its sharpest when his wife slept on her side with her back to him. In mounting excitement, M would rub against her and want to make love when she was still not quite awake. If, however, the wife gave intimation of becoming an enthusiastic partner in the exercise, M sometimes ejaculated prematurely or found his erection precipitately shrivel.

It is evident from these brief fragments of M's case history that his desire is closely connected with some of the most inert parts of a woman's body, hips and buttocks. In other words, the desire needs the woman to be sexually dead for its fulfillment. The genesis of the fantasy of the hanging corpse with whom M has intercourse at night has at its root the fear of the mother's sexuality as well as the anger at their restraint on his explorations of the world. My choice of M's case, though, is not dictated by the interest it may hold from a psychoanalytical perspective. The choice, instead, has to do with its central theme, namely the various paths in imagination which M traverses, in the face of many obstacles, to maintain an idealized relationship with the maternal body. This theme and the fantasized solutions to the disorders in the mother–son relationship are repeated again and again in Indian case and life histories. Bose's observation on the Indian male patient's "primitive idea of being a woman" is then only a special proposition of a more general theorem.

The wish to be a woman is one particular solution to the discord that threatens the breaking up of the son's fantasized connection to the mother, a solution whose access to awareness is facilitated by the culture's views on sexual differentiation and the permeability of gender boundaries. Thus, for instance, when Gandhi (1958) publicly proclaims that he has mentally become a woman or, quite unaware of Karen

Horney and other deviants from the orthodox analytic position of the time, talks of man's envy of the woman's procreative capacities, saying "There is as much reason for a man to wish that he was born a woman as for woman to do otherwise" (p. 13), he is sure of a sympathetic and receptive audience.

Unconsciously absorbed since childhood, it is our culture that determines what it means to be, look, think, or behave like a man or a woman. This becomes clearer if one thinks of Greek or Roman sculpture with their hard, muscled men's bodies and chests without any fat at all, familiar to most Europeans from childhood visits to museums or reproduced in countless visual mediums, and one compares it with the sculpted representations of Hindu gods in the temples or the Buddha, where the bodies are softer, suppler, and, in their hint of breasts, nearer to the female form. Between a minimum of sexual differentiation needed to function heterosexually with a modicum of pleasure and a maximum which cuts off any sense of empathy and emotional contact with the other sex experienced as a different species altogether, there is a whole range of positions, each occupied by a culture that assumes it is universal and insists on calling it the only one that is mature and healthy.

In the Indian context, the theme of maternal enthrallment can be explored in individual stories as well as in cultural narratives we call myths, both of which are more closely interwoven in Indian culture than is the case in the modern West. In an apparent reversal of a Western pattern, traditional myths in India are less a source of intellectual and aesthetic satisfaction for the mythologist than of emotional recognition for others, more moving for the patient than for the analyst. Myths in India are not part of a bygone era. They are not "retained fragments from the infantile psychic life of the race" as Karl Abraham (1909, p. 72) called them, or "vestiges of the infantile fantasies of whole nations, secular dreams of youthful humanity" in Freud's words (Freud, 1908e, p. 152). Vibrantly alive, their symbolic power intact, Indian myths constitute a cultural idiom which aids the individual in the construction and integration of his inner world. Parallel to patterns of infant care and to the structure and values of family relationships, popular and well-known myths are isomorphic with the central psychological constellations of the culture and are constantly renewed and validated by the nature of subjective experience (Obeyesekere, 1981). Given the availability of the mythological idiom, it is almost as easy to mythologize a psychoanalysis, such as that of M, as to analyse a myth; almost as convenient to elaborate on intrapsychic conflict in a mythological mode as it is in the narrative mode of a case history.

Earlier, I advanced the thesis that the myths of Devi, the great goddess, constitute a "hegemonic narrative" of Hindu Indian culture. Of the hundreds of myths on her various manifestations, my special interest here is in the goddess as mother, and especially the mother of the sons, Ganesha and Skanda. But before proceeding to connect M's tale to the larger cultural story, let me note that I have ignored the various versions of these myths in traditional texts and modern folklore—an undertaking which is rightly the preserve of mythologists and folklorists—and instead picked on their best-known, popular versions.

The popularity of Ganesha and Skanda as gods—psychologically representing two childhood positions of the Indian son—is certainly undeniable. Ganesha, the remover of obstacles and the god of all beginnings, is perhaps the most adored of the reputed 330 million Hindu gods. Iconically represented as a pot-bellied toddler with an elephant head and one missing tusk, he is represented proportionately as a small child when portrayed in the family group with his mother Parvati and father Shiva. His image, whether carved in stone or drawn up in a colored print, is everywhere: in temples, homes, shops, roadside shrines, calendars. Ganesha's younger brother, Skanda or Kartikkeya, has his own following, especially in south India where he is extremely popular and worshipped under the name of Murugan or Subramanya. In contrast to Ganesh, Skanda is a handsome child, a youth of slender body and heroic exploits who in analytic parlance may be said to occupy the phallic position.

Ganesha's myths tell us one part of M's inner life while those of Skanda reveal yet another. Ganesha, in many myths, is solely his mother Parvati's creation. Desirous of a child and lacking Shiva's co-operation in the venture, she created him out of the dirt and sweat of her body mixed with unguents. Like M's fantasies of his femininity, Ganesha too is not only his mother's boy but contains her very essence. Even when indubitably male like Skanda, M is immersed in the world of mothers which an Indian extended family creates for the child. Skanda, like M, is the son of more than one mother; his father Shiva's seed being too powerful could not be borne by one woman and wandered from womb to womb before Skanda was given life. M's ravenous consumption of sweets to restore feelings of well-being has parallels with Ganesha's appetite for modakas, the sweet wheat or rice balls which devotees offer to the god in large quantities, "knowing" that the god is never satisfied, that his belly empties itself as fast as it is filled (Courtright, 1986, p. 114). For, like the lean M, the fat god's sweets are a lifeline to the mother's breast; his hunger for the mother's body, in spite of temporary appeasements, is ultimately doomed to remain unfulfilled. M is further like Ganesha in that he too has emerged from infancy with an ample capacity for vital involvement with others.

In the dramatization of M's dilemma in relation to the mother, brought to a head by developmental changes that push the child toward an exploration of the outer world while they also give him increasing intimations of his biological rock-bottom identity as a male, Ganesha and Skanda play the leading roles. In a version common to both south India and Sri Lanka (Obeyesekere, 1984) the myth goes as follows:

> A mango was floating down the stream and Uma (Parvati), the mother, said that whoever rides around the universe first will get the mango [in other versions, the promise is of modakas or wives]. Skanda impulsively got on his golden peacock and went around the universe. But Ganesha, who rode the rat, had more wisdom. He thought: "What could my mother have meant by this?" He then circumambulated his mother, worshipped her and said, "I have gone around my universe." Since Ganesha was right his mother gave him the mango. Skanda was furious when he arrived and demanded the mango. But before he could get it, Ganesha bit the mango and broke one of his tusks. (p. 471)

Here Skanda and Ganesha are personifications of the two opposing wishes of the older child on the eve of what analysts have called the oedipal phase. He is torn between a powerful push for independent and autonomous functioning and an equally strong pull toward surrender and re-immersion in the enveloping maternal fusion from which he has just emerged. Giving in to the pull of individuation and independence, Skanda becomes liable to one kind of punishment—exile from the mother's bountiful presence—and one kind of reward—the promise of functioning as an adult, virile man. Going back to the mother—and I would view Ganesha's eating of the mango as a return to and feeding at the breast, especially since we know that in Tamil Nadu the analogy between a mango and the breast is a matter of common awareness (Egnor, 1986, p. 45)—has the broken tusk, the loss of potential masculinity, as a consequence. Remaining an infant, Ganesha's reward, on the other hand, will be never to know the pangs of separation from the mother, never to feel the despair at her absence. That Ganesha's lot is considered superior to Skanda's is perhaps an indication of Indian man's cultural preference in the dilemma of separation–individuation. He is at one with his mother in her wish not to have the son separate from her; individuate out of their shared anima (Kakar, 1987b).

While the Indian cultural imagination does not doubt the *reality* of separation, it refuses to admit that separation–individuation is the highest level of reality. Instead, the Indian vision of reality emphasizes union and oneness. Consider here, the Punjabi proverb about death: "It is like being shifted from one breast of the mother to the other. The child feels lost for that instant, but not for long." What stands out in this proverb is that it is the continuation of breastfeeding rather than the aspirations of weaning and the independence implicit in weaning that dominates the Indian imagination. Thus one might speak here too, as I did earlier about gender, about the existence of a range of psychic positions. Between a minimum of separation–individuation needed to function as an adult in a particular society, and a maximum which encases a person in a narcissistic armor, cutting off all ties with family and community, there is a range of positions, all of which need to be recognized by psychoanalysis as part of being human rather than closely identifying with any particular position on the continuum as the only one that is "healthy and mature."

For M, as we have seen, the Ganesha position is often longed for and sometimes returned to in fantasy. It does not, however, represent an enduring solution to the problem of maintaining phallic desire in the face of the overwhelming inner presence of the Great Mother. Enter Skanda. After he killed the demon Taraka who had been terrorizing the gods, the goddess became quite indulgent toward her son and told him to amuse himself as he pleased. Skanda became wayward, his lust rampant.

He made love to the wives of the gods and the gods could not stop him. On their complaining to the goddess, she decided to take the form of whatever woman Skanda was about to seduce. Skanda summoned the wife of one god after another but in each saw his mother and became passionless. Finally thinking that "the universe is filled with my mother" he decided to remain celibate for ever.

M, too, we saw, became "passionless" whenever in the bus the motherly woman he fancied turned to face him. But, instead of celibacy, he tried to hold on to desire by killing the sexual part of the mother, deadening the lower portion of her trunk, which threatened him with impotence. Furthermore, the imagined sexual overpowering-ness of the mother, in the face of which the child feels hopelessly inadequate, with fears of being engulfed and swallowed by her dark depths, is not experienced by M in the form of clear-cut fantasies but in a recurrent nightmare from which he wakes up screaming.

The conflict around survival and destruction of the overwhelming mother, the second aspect of maternal enthrallment, is manifested in another popular myth that is associated with one of the most popular gods of Hinduism, Krishna, the incarnation of Vishnu. He is said to have been born to rid the earth of the tyranny and oppression of King Kamsa. According to the myth, Kamsa, informed of the prophecy that the eighth child of his uncle's daughter would one day slay him, confined his cousin and her husband in a prison and killed all their offspring as soon as they were born. But Krishna, the eighth child, was smuggled out of the prison and taken to live with foster parents in another part of the kingdom. Kamsa, learning of the infant Krishna's escape and yet ignorant of his exact whereabouts, instructed the demoness Putana to kill all the boys born in the kingdom during the month his cousin had expected the birth of her child. Putana went around the kingdom, obediently carrying out her master's orders. Transformed into a beautiful young woman, with a deadly poison smeared on her nipples, she finally came to Krishna's house. Pretending an upsurge of maternal love she took Krishna from his foster mother and gave him her poisoned breast to suckle. Krishna suckled so hard that he not only drank all the milk Putana had to give but also sucked her life away. The maternal monster fell dead, with Krishna's mouth still at her breast. The legend concludes that Putana nevertheless attained salvation since she had acted as a mother, albeit a malevolent one, to the infant god.

From the Kleinian echoes of the Putana legend, let us go to incestuous reverberations of maternal enthrallment in a Kannada folk narrative (Ramanujan, 1999, pp. 518–530), a tale from the "little traditions" as compared to the "great" tradition of Sanskrit myths on the origins of civilization.

The primal goddess, Adishakti, is born three days before the rest of her creation. When she attains puberty she finds there is no man to pleasure her. She creates Brahma and asks him to sleep with her. "How can I do that? You are my mother!" Brahma replies. She is angry and burns him to ashes. Next day she creates Vishnu and asks him the same question. His refusal is followed by the same consequences. On the third day, she gives birth to Shiva. At first, Shiva too refuses her incestuous offer. She threatens: "My hands have the power to create worlds, and the power to burn them down." Shiva asks her to let him grow up first. Growing into youth, he learns her powers of creation and destruction from her. On her importuning for sex, Shiva finally tells her that he will sleep with her if she dances the powerful dance of cosmic destruction with him and wins. She agrees but through a stratagem Shiva sets her on fire and reduces her to ashes. Dying, she curses Shiva, "He refused a woman, so may his body be stuck with the very kind of female he refused"—which takes us to the ardhanarishwara, half-man, half-woman, form of Shiva.

Once the mother is gone Shiva revives his brothers Brahma and Vishnu and the cosmos is recreated. To give birth to human beings, women are needed. Shiva goes to the heap of ashes of his mother, and creates consorts for the three gods by dividing the ashes of the mother … civilization founded on matricide.

I am aware that in the great Sanskrit tradition, the creation myth has father–daughter incest, or near incest, as the defining moment of creation. Parricide, though, is almost completely absent in both myths and folklore and this brings us to the question: what about the father?

He is at the periphery of the dyad, hovering in the background, a barely palpable presence, yet nonetheless vital for muting the overwhelming presence of an engulfing or sexually threatening mother.

The demon Mahisasura had conquered all the three worlds. Falling in love with the goddess Devi, Shiva's wife, he sent a message to make his desire known to her. Devi replied that she would accept as her husband only someone who defeated her in battle. Mahisasura entered the battlefield with a vast demon army and a huge quantity of fighting equipment. Devi came alone, mounted on her lion. The gods were surprised to see her without even armour, riding naked into combat. Dismounting, Devi started dancing and cutting off the heads of millions and millions of demons with her sword, to the rhythm of her movement. Mahisasura, facing death, tried to run away by becoming an elephant. Devi cut off his trunk. The elephant became a buffalo and against its thick hide Devi's sword and spear were of no avail. Angered, Devi jumped on the buffalo's back and rode it to exhaustion. When the buffalo demon's power of resistance had collapsed, Devi plunged her spear into its ear and Mahisasura fell dead.

The myth is stark enough in its immediacy and needs no further gloss on the omnipotence and sexual energy of the goddess, expressed in the imagery of her dancing and riding naked, exhausting even the most powerful male to abject submission and ultimately death.

The myth continues. When Devi's frenzied dancing did not come to an end, even after the killing of the buffalo demon, the gods became alarmed and asked Shiva for help. Shiva lay down on his back and when the goddess stepped on her husband (Shiva), she hung out her tongue in shame and stopped. Shiva enters the scene supine, yet a container for the great mother goddess' energy and power. In other words, the father may be unassuming and remote, but powerful. First experienced as a wished-for ally and a protector, the father rarely emerges as a rival in myths and folklore. Where it does occur, the rivalry in popular Indian myths and most of the case histories is not so much that of Oedipus, where the power of the myth derives from the son's guilt over a fantasized and eventually unconscious parricide; the Indian context stresses more the father's envy of what belongs to the son—especially the mother—and thus the son's persecution anxiety as a primary motivation in the father–son relationship. This comes through clearly in another Ganesha myth.

In this particular myth, Ganesha was created solely by his mother, Parvati, from her bodily substances. (Parvati's husband, Shiva, was away for a long time, busy doing penance on the mountain, so Parvati, using her own power, conceived her son, Ganesha. Consequently, the father and the son never met each other.) One day, when Parvati was taking a bath, she instructed the little boy, Ganesha, to stand guard outside the door and let no one in. While the boy was standing guard, his "father," Lord Shiva, returned from his penance and asked the boy to step aside so he could visit his wife. Ganesha, following his mother's strict instructions, refused. Enraged, Lord Shiva cut off his head. Hearing the commotion, Parvati came outside. Seeing her son lying dead, Parvati was furious and inconsolable. Shiva promised to restore the boy to life and ordered a servant to go out and bring back the first head he found, so Shiva could replace the boy's head. The servant brought the first head he found, that of an elephant. That is how Ganesha came to have a little boy's body and an elephant's head.[6]

In most myths and legends, though, the rivalry between father and son centers on the *father's* attempt to defy generational barriers rather than the son's wishes for sexual union with the mother.

The king Santanu, Bhishma's father falls in love with a fisher girl. He goes to the girl's father to ask for her hand. The fisherman agrees to the match on the condition that the son born to his daughter inherit the kingdom. Santanu cannot give his consent to this condition. He returns to his palace where he sinks into a depression born of an old man's unfulfilled passion for a young girl. Bhishma, on coming to know the reason for his father's grief, goes to the fisherman. Bhishma promises both the renunciation of the kingdom and of sexual life that could result in a progeny threatening the rights of the sons born to the fisher girl.

King Yayati, cursed by a sage to suffer old age, wants to live a life of sensual pleasure and asks his five sons, one after another, to give him their youth for a thousand years. The four elder sons refuse and are cursed by the father. Puru, the youngest son agrees. "Take my youth from me and enjoy the pleasures you are seeking," he says. "Covered with your old age and wearing your aged body, I shall live as you say

---

[6] Filicide is also characteristic of the most popular Iranian legend of father–son relations, that of Rustam and Sohrab. In this legend, one of the Persian culture's "master narratives," it is the son and not the father who is killed in the father–son conflict when the father Rustam does not recognize the son Sohrab on the battlefield. The Iranian Oedipus, too, thus has a different outcome from the oedipal myth, filicide rather than parricide, although it is still central to the organization of a boy's object relations.

and give you my youth." Puru is blessed by the father and later inherits the kingdom.

These myths have the son's self-castration that sacrifices to the father the son's right to sexual activity and generational ascendancy. The son does so in order to deflect the father's envy and his primal fear of annihilation at the father's hands while keeping the bond of love between father and son intact.

These myths, as also the one on Ganesha's beheading, are part of a plethora of Indian narratives that invert the psychoanalytically postulated causality between the fantasies of parricide and filicide. They are charged with the fear of filicide rather than the oedipal guilt of parricide. They stress the father's envy[7] and thus the son's persecution anxiety as the primary motivation in Hindu Indian culture.

With exceptions (e.g., I. Levy, 2011; J. M. Ross, 1982), psychoanalysis has seriously underestimated the father's envy and rivalry with the son (as of the mother with the daughter). The Indian legends show how formidable an oedipal rival the son remains to the father, a rival who, in the Indian cultural imagination, has never been fully conquered or is even experienced as the victor in the oedipal struggle. If Indian cultural imagination is at pains to emphasise the "good father," the Eros between father and son, as in the following vignettes, then it is partly also to deflect from the father's destructive envy of the son.

In the epic *Mahabharata* which, along with the Ramayana, continues to be a repository of Hindu Indian cultural imagination, Shakuntla says to King Dushyanta (*Mahabharata*, Book 1, 1973):

> A son stumbles and covered with dust embraces his father—is there a joy beyond that? ... Neither clothes nor loving women nor water are so good to touch as the infant son you embrace. Of two-footed men the Brahmin is best; of four-footed beasts the cow is worthiest; of respected men the guru is the first; and of all things to touch a son is the choicest. Embrace and touch your handsome son! There is no feeling on earth lovelier than to feel a son. (pp. 167–168)

---

[7] "He [the son] is a new male: his growth is his father's decline, his youth his father's envy, his friend his father's enemy" (James Joyce, *Ulysses*).

Or in Uttara Ramayana Charita, the Indian culture hero, King Rama, meeting his grown-up son for the first time, says, "Let me fold thee again and again in a close embrace. Soft and smooth and tender like the mellowed interior of a full-blown lotus, and cool like the moon or like the juice of sandal thy touch fills me with joy."

In the son, if there is anger against the father then it is due to his distance and failure in not fulfilling the little boy's need for an oedipal alliance, that is, for the father's firm support, solidarity, and emotional availability at a stage of life where the dangers of maternal enthrallment were at their peak. In the clinic, the male longing for the oedipal alliance—the inverse of a rivalrous father—and the terror of female sexuality is reflected in the following vignette from a longer case history (Kakar, 1997, pp. 82–87).

Case study 3

Karan was a forty-year-old lecturer at a university who came to therapy suffering from severe anxiety states. He was the firstborn of a middle-class family in Jaipur that had gone through great financial difficulties when he was in high school although it had later recovered its fortunes. Karan's portrait of his father was of an imperious patriarch who worked hard, had strict moral standards, but was quite distant from his two sons when they were growing up. Children, the father felt, were a woman's business and he rarely concerned himself with their upbringing. Karan remembered his mother as a beautiful woman, somewhat dreamy and quite self-absorbed. Outwardly a submissive housewife, Karan's mother seemed to have lived in her own imaginary world while the son looked on, fearful and adoring, but always at the edge of her closed world. Overprotective of the child at times and quite indifferent at others, the solipsistic world of the mother baffled the child who could be included and banished at whim.

In adolescence, it seems, from the ages of fourteen to eighteen, Karan had incestuous experiences with his mother. Since the family was living in a single room at the time, Karan would lie in the same bed with his mother on many hot afternoons while his father was away at work. While his mother pretended to be asleep, Karan would gingerly rub his penis against the back of his mother thighs and ejaculate in his pyjamas. In the analytic sessions, memories came up which made it evident that Karan's mother was not a passive recipient of the boy's sexual advances—as Karan wanted to believe—but in fact actively encouraged the son. She would ask Karan to lock the door against the father's unexpected return and often contrived to lie in bed in a way that pulled her sari above her thighs. In one of the sessions that produced pronounced anxiety, Karan recalled that after he had ejaculated, his mother said to him, "You satisfy yourself, but you should also take care of me."

With the activation of memories of his mother's seductiveness, Karan also began to discover intense rage toward her at the same time that his idealization of me in the transference became more marked, his efforts to identify with me more insistent. Lying on the couch, he would often turn his face to look at me, as if reassuring himself of my continued presence, searching for a father who would not only not punish but also help him contain his fear and rage against an overwhelming, threatening mother. His search for the oedipal alliance is epitomized in one particular session in which Karan began with a parapraxis, "I had an erotic mother"—instead of "I had an erotic dream." He then described the dream:

I am lying on my bed when I see my mother approaching, She is almost naked and has a gloating expression on her face. I am very scared. Then I see you (the analyst) with an enormous erect penis next to you that reaches from the floor to the ceiling. I hold the penis in my arms and feel safe.

My own associations to Karan's dream took me to a mythological motif, depicted in the reliefs on many temple walls, in which a boy holds on to a Shiva lingam-phallus—to escape Yama, the god of death; in Karan's case, the god of death is a (mother-) goddess.[8]

Another patient with a long history of depression accompanied by spells of impotence, soon after getting married, dreamt:

I am in our village home when a gang of dacoits led by a girl, attack our house. The female leader of the band is chasing me through the rooms of the house. I pass my father in the hall. He is lying on the bed with a gun but his gun is ineffective. I am very afraid as

---

[8] I will explore the motif of the Shiva lingam, ubiquitous in Hindu cultural imagination, more fully in Chapter 6.

the female bandit runs after me, laughing and mocking me for not being able to defend myself. (Kakar, 1997, p. 82)

A failure of the oedipal alliance where the father, unlike the supine Shiva with the Goddess Durga, is helpless to contain a rampaging mother.

Female development

In contrast to the son, the maternal enthrallment of the daughter is given short shrift in Indian cultural imagination. Myths, legends, and other popular narratives generally ignore the mother–daughter dyad. As observed earlier (Kakar, 1978), "in a patriarchal culture myths are inevitably man-made and man-oriented. Addressing as they do the unconscious wishes and fears of men, it is the parent–son rather than the parent–daughter relationships which become charged with symbolic significance" (p. 57). With one exception: the mother–daughter rivalry and the daughter's fears of retribution. Given the massive idealisation of mothers in the culture, the envious mother, A. K. Ramanujan (1999) reminds us, is always costumed as a mother-in-law. Narratives of barren queen mothers who fight with their young daughters-in-law are plentiful in folk tales all over India, and these altercations are, Ramanujan asserts "blatantly for sexual success with the king" (p. 391). In a rare example of a clear mother–daughter rivalry, one Kannada folk tale speaks of a mother so rivalrous of her daughter's beauty that she puts a clay-mask over the young girl's face (Ramanujan, 1999, p. 361). In the clinic, the daughter's fantasy of maternal envy and retribution is always partially in disguise: it shows up as women's sexual self-suppression (Narayanan, 2013, 2018, 2023), the counterpart of the son's renouncing of sexual agency as in the Bhishma and Yayati myths. It also comes into view in the clinic, the psychoanalyst Honey Oberoi (2019) tells us, in extended, even excessive, periods of mourning for mothers' erotic losses that must be lived out before a girl's erotic life can begin. Oberoi also argues that a preoccupation with the mother, what I call maternal enthrallment, is as much the lot of girls as of boys. If we accept Oberoi's clinical testimony, then the psychoanalytic focus on the bad mother, and maternal ambivalence, while necessary, represses mother-love—including the homosexual dimension of mother-love.

And the father? Within the atmosphere of a general avoidance of close contact with men as a consequence of the segregation of the sexes that takes place in both urban and rural areas after the girl crosses the ages of eight or nine, there is one poignant dimension: the little time a daughter spends with her father and especially the culturally enjoined cessation of any physical contact between the father and the daughter as she enters puberty. I imagine that this prohibition of physical contact between father and daughter also has a source in the cultural imagination where myths that narrate the father's desire for his daughter are easily found in ancient Indian texts. Prajapati—elsewhere identified as Brahma, the Creator[9]—is described in the Śatapatha Brāhmana as casting his eyes upon his own daughter and saying "May I pair with her?" (Ramanujan, 1999, p. 388). When he consummates his desire, Prajapati is punished by the other gods: his body is pierced through. Numerous versions of this myth reflected in other ancient myths as well as folk tales narrate the untrustworthy nature of the father's desire and the need for forces outside the family to step in to protect the daughter from the father's lust. The mother is never the protective force—that role is reserved for other men—but it is worth wondering that as much as the son requires an oedipal alliance to protect him from overwhelming femaleness, the daughter too requires an oedipal alliance with the mother to protect her from the overwhelming nature of her father's desire.

The absent father at this stage of a growing girl's life has been called "one of the great tragedies of Indian family life" (Anandalakshmi, 1994). My notes on the first three sessions of a psychoanalytic therapy with an urban, professional young woman can perhaps convey some of the subjective experience of this psychic "tragedy."

Case study 4

Meera is a twenty-eight-year-old advertising copywriter who feels depressed most of the time, empty and bereft of ideas at work, and unable to form relationships.

---

[9] The Hindu trinity consists of Brahma, the Creator, Vishnu, the Preserver, and Shiva, the Destroyer.

First session. After she lies down on the couch
We are both silent for a couple of minutes although I imagine the silence seems much longer to her as she starts becoming anxious, the mix of hope and fear with which a patient begins an analysis sliding into the latter. The silence heralds the shift in the inner space that is taking place in both of us. I can feel wisps of her anxiety floating through this space in my own body: in the stirring of the follicles of hair on my forearms, in the reflexively swallowing motion of my gullet. This is our first shared silence and I know that over the years we will experience its many varieties: silences that will be companionable, others of deep attunement, or ones tingling with erotic energy. But also silences in which she will try to cast me out, become withdrawn and sad or resentful and angry and yet, if the therapy has gone well, leave an opening for me to engage her again. But this is the beginning, our first silence that should only lead her away from the spaces of ordinary life and not traumatize her. This is the very first session and I do not have a feel for how much anxious silence she can bear.

"What are you thinking?" I ask her in a friendly voice.

The question is less about her thoughts and more an invitation to her to find words out of the silence, to build a bridge from the unsaid, perhaps even the unsayable, words that fortify the connection that has begun to be forged between us even before she has spoken. She does not reply at once.

The thumb and fingers of her right hand are playing with the beads of the thin gold chain around her neck. Her eyes are closed.

"I am in a paddy field," she begins in English. "There is a low bund going through the field and you are on the other side. I step over the bund to you."

She waits and then switches to Hindi.

"There was a pleasant feeling to the dream," she says.

"A paddy field?" I say musingly to both of us.

She takes ownership of my pensive query.

"Our family had paddy fields when I was a child. I remember walking with my father on the narrow mud embankments separating the fields. I would hold on tightly to his hand so that I didn't slip on the wet earth and fall into the flooded field. I remember my father overseeing the women planting the seedlings. Bending down from the waist, their saris pulled up to the waist, their legs exposed, the women sometimes sang. We would listen to the song for a while before we returned home."

I feel the sadness in her voice. Inchoate memories, without words, of the losses in my own life begin to stir.

"It all changed after my twelfth birthday. My father became distant. He no longer took me with him on his tours of the fields. I could no longer hold his hand. He would stop me from giving him a hug. 'No more embraces. You will soon be a woman. You have to learn to be modest, restrained in your girlish behaviour.' My mother would get a fit if I walked around the house in a skirt and not a sari. 'What will the servants say?'"

I am aware that she has also dreamt this dream for me. Indeed, all dreams of a patient during an analysis, or even shortly before starting one, are dreams she dreams both for herself and for the analyst, whether or not he figures explicitly in them. I let the dream swirl in my mind, like a cube of ice in a single malt whisky (to which I am partial) before taking the first sip. I have taken her dream as mine. I dream her dream of hope and fear.

"It seems the dream is telling us of your hope in the work we are about to begin together ... the tender shoots of paddy that have been planted, your feeling of well-being as you cross over to me. Bund in Hindi means closed but there is reassurance in the dream that the way is not closed, but open," I say.

My interpretation of Meera's dream is at a basic level, more in service of creating a relationship, deepening our connection, than an insight that surprises her. It is but one thread in the weaving of her story that will feel true to both of us. For as she spoke and I let my mind wander in the landscape of her dream, there were other meanings also jostling for attention. The first sentence, "I am in a paddy field" was in English. Meera did her BA in English literature from the capital's Lady Shriram College before taking a course in commercial art. "To be in a paddy" is British slang for being in fit of temper, raging. At the father for turning away so precipitately from the girl who was becoming a woman? I sense her hope that I will repair the damage caused by her father's withdrawal, rid her of the noxious rage but also her warning that I could be its target whenever my image in her imagination becomes fused with that of the rejecting father of her teens.

Third session

Almost at its end, after we have been silent for a while. Her silence is brimming with the unsaid. I can feel her struggle between words, simultaneously reluctant to leave the refuge of silence and in their wish to communicate with me. The balance finally shifts in favor of speech.

"There was something else in the dream I told you about the first time I came. Besides you is a round pillar that comes up to your waist, like a Shiva lingam. It has an odd colour, more of brick than stone. I have an urge to kneel down and hold it."

I become aware of noises from outside the room: a rickshaw with a defective muffler passing on the road, the dhobi/washerman next to my house who has set up a stall on the footpath for ironing clothes scolding his teenage daughter. Furtively, I look at my wrist watch. There are still ten minutes left till the end of the session. I realize that the shift in my attention is due to my reluctance to engage with this fresh image of Meera's dream. I close my eyes.

The outside noises recede and wisps of my earlier state of reverie begin to trail into my consciousness. An image floats up.

"There is the story of a boy, a great worshipper of Lord Shiva who flung his arms around a Shiva lingam and clung tightly to it when Yama came to take him. Defeated, the god of death had to go back empty handed," I say.

In choosing to view the phallus solely as one of grey or black stone, of Shiva, Meera is colluding with me, picking up on the meaning I have assigned to the lingam of her dream.

"Isn't there another version that when Yama tried to pull the boy off, the lingam broke. Shiva was so angry at the damage to the lingam that he cursed Yama that he will no longer be able to carry out his assigned task. Since no one died anymore, the world became overpopulated and Shiva soon had to take his curse back."

I muse to myself, though not exactly in the words I write here, that we equate death with a self stripped of all memories, stretching back to infancy, of which the most vital are of persons we have loved and who have loved us. What we fear is less the end of the body than the end of all our relationships, past and present, which constitute the mind. What we sense in death is its inconceivable loneliness, a desolation of psychotic proportions. Meera has imbued the lingam of her dream, a phallus which is both mine and not mine, with a godlike power that can keep at bay the unimaginable dread of a self that is empty of all ties. I think I understand my own disquiet. Perhaps I have sensed that there are deeper terrors, of total abandonment, underlying her presenting symptoms.

CHAPTER 3

The analyst and the mystic-guru: Siblings or strangers?

The psychoanalytic presumption of an unbridgeable gulf between psychoanalysis and the Indian mystical traditions, embodied by the figure of the guru, is of special interest to an Indian psychoanalyst. Unlike his Western counterpart, the Indian analyst has at some time or the other consciously faced and reflected on the conflict between an absorbing intellectual orientation—psychoanalysis—which is the mainstay of his professional identity, and the working of a historical fate which has made the "mystical" the distinctive leitmotif of his Indian cultural tradition and thus a part of his cultural imagination.

Let me begin with what is common to both mysticism and psychoanalysis. They are both ways of inner transformation. The mystical path, of course, is the more ancient, universal, and highly regarded even when in many countries at different historical times its practitioners have often lived in an uneasy truce, if not frank antagonism, with the established religion of their societies. What divides psychoanalysis and mysticism are their diverging goals of inner transformation, what that transformation must look like.

First, take the goal of psychoanalysis. The psychoanalytic goal is to lead to an outcome where the person, through an increased self-understanding by making the unconscious conscious, attains a freedom to love, work, and play, free from inhibitions her mind has gathered over the life cycle, especially the childhood years. One can also say one of the aims of psychoanalysis is increasing a person's choices. It is important to note that essential to psychoanalysis is a view that the process of self-understanding, or what it calls insight, of coming to know oneself or even of attempting to do so, is the unique satisfaction that psychoanalytic therapy has to offer.

Coming to mysticism, we usually equate mysticism with what I would call the peak mystical experience. The peak experience is said to be characterized by an expansion of consciousness that also fills the external world which appears to be pervaded by a oneness of existence. The overwhelming feeling is of the world having at last become transparent and more real than its conventional reality. All of this is accompanied by heightened bodily sensations and a great feeling of pleasure or rather bliss, ananda, which absorbs all other experience. Variously called cosmic consciousness, peak experience, mahabhava, it is the samadhi of the Hindus, satori of Zen Buddhism, fana of the Sufis.

Is there nothing common here between psychoanalysis and mysticism? I think there is if we view mysticism not only in terms of a peak experience but as a mountain climb with many base camps marking progress on the way. The first camp from which one cannot see the summit, covered as it is by clouds, though we know it is there, is tolerance, defined minimally as giving the benefit of the doubt to others. The second camp, a little higher, can be said to be compassion, while the third and the last camp from where one climbs to the summit is empathy, the "feeling into" another person, although of course, empathy can also encompass a "feeling into" nature. The point is that the mystical climb fosters deeper and deeper feelings of connectedness, although only a few, rare saints can reach the summit, the peak experience, expressed in the Upanishadic ideal of "he who sees all beings in his own self and his own self in all beings." Most of us can consider ourselves fortunate if we can catch a glimpse of the peak from the base camps of tolerance, compassion, and empathy. We need to recognize that in this sense psychoanalysis too is a spiritual climb in so far as it makes these base camps accessible, even when it prefers to stop short of or negates the existence of a summit.

In spite of the respect granted to a few analysts such as Bion who is considered sympathetic to the mystic, if not a closet mystic himself (Grotstein, 1981), and of mystical states being considered as integrative and adaptive by a few analysts (Brickman, 1998; Eigen, 1981, 2001; Epstein, 1990; Fromm, 1960; Horton, 1974; Meissner, 1984; Shaffi, 1973; Werman, 1986), psychoanalysts have generally embraced some version of Freud's (1930a) dismissive view of the mystical "oceanic feeling" of unity with the cosmos as the limitless primary narcissism of the infant united with the mother at the breast (Alexander, 1931; Fingarette, 1958; Masson, 1980; N. Ross, 1975). I believe this indifference at best and hostility at worst, at least toward the Indian guru-mystic, has two sources: one, the history of psychoanalysis and two, an insufficient understanding of the Indian guru-mystics and how they differ from their Western counterparts, notably the Christian mystic-saints.

If we except the Jungians, there is a venerable psychoanalytic tradition going back to Freud (1927c) that tends to view mysticism as part of the religious-spiritual domain of experience that is incompatible with analytic thought. And although today we distinguish between the religious and the spiritual, a distinction that was first made in nineteenth-century USA by such writers and poets as Ralph Waldo Emerson and Walt Whitman, the smell of religion continues to cling to the term. Religion and spirituality are not synonyms even if they are often regarded as such by many who have been brought up in the Judeo-Christian worldview. The religious belief in God may be of great help in the striving for spiritual progress but it is not a necessity. In many Hindu and Buddhist psycho-philosophical schools, an experiential understanding of the "true" nature of the self is sought through an intensive practice of certain meditative-contemplative disciplines which do not require the presence of religious belief. In the Hindu Upanishadic and Yogic mysticism, for example, there is no trace of love or yearning for communion with God which is considered the highest manifestation of spiritual mood in the Christian and Islamic mystical traditions (as also in the Hindu *bhakti* devotionalism), without which no spiritual illumination is conceivable. Buddhist practices, too, are silent on the question of a Divine Being.

In many Indian traditions, then, spiritual progress is achieved entirely through the seeker's own efforts and without the intervention of divine grace. In other words, Indian mysticism traditions have many of what have been called "self-power approaches," in contrast to the "other-power" approaches that are fueled by religious faith (Safran, 2016). Mystical disciplines regard themselves as scientific in the sense that they describe the stages and processes of transformation of consciousness through the prescribed practices of certain disciplines under the supervision of an adept, the guru. And, indeed, their descriptions of mental states reached through meditative practices are no longer solely dependent on subjective but credible reports of advanced practitioners, through the ages, but have begun to gather support from brain research in the emerging discipline of "neurotheology" (Newberg, 2018).

It seems to me that one cause for the friction between psychoanalysis and mysticism arises from the fact that they essentially cultivate the same field—the self—and with not dissimilar methods that attempt to look inwards. Mutual irritation is bound to follow as the two keep on bumping against each other. Historically, the psychoanalytic practice of healing what was called "soul disturbances," *Seelenstoerungen*, was too near that of numerous occultists and faith healers who operated at the fringes of the established churches in Europe. The psychoanalytic method was too close to older introspective techniques that drew their sustenance from religion. As late as 1931, the Austrian writer Stefan Zweig (1931) apologetically wrote that he hopes he won't be accused of being a Mesmerist or a Christian Scientist or a devotee of psycho-analysis. Craving respectability as a science, it is understandable that psychoanalysis would seek to sharply demarcate its boundaries and differentiate its methods from comparable spiritual techniques that antedate it so vastly in the history of human consciousness.

Besides the vagaries of history and the imperatives of its own evolution, I believe the antipathy of psychoanalysis toward mysticism has been largely precipitated by their different worldviews.

The psychoanalytic worldview or its "vision of reality" (Schaefer, 1970) is primarily a tragic one. It is tragic in so far as it sees human experience pervaded by uncertainties and absurdities where man has little choice but to bear the burden of unanswerable questions, inescapable conflicts, and incomprehensible afflictions of fate. Life in this vision is a linear movement which cannot be undone; many wishes remain fated to be unfulfilled and ungratified. On the other hand, the Indian mystical vision of reality offers a romantic quest, a goal. Life's journey is a search and the seeker, if he withstands all the perils of the road, will be rewarded by an exaltation beyond normal human experience, an access to a "higher" consciousness than the one mediated by our senses.

Trapped in their respective visions of reality, psychoanalysts and mystics have generally shown a mutual disdain. If Freud saw the mystical "oceanic feeling" of unity with the cosmos as the limitless primary narcissism of the infant united with the mother at the breast, a highly esteemed Indian mystic, Sri Aurobindo, peevishly observed that he finds it "difficult to take psychoanalysis seriously," that "one cannot discover the meaning of the lotus by the secrets of the mud in which it grows," and that as a science psychoanalysis is in "its infancy—inconsiderate, awkward and rudimentary at one and same time" (Servadio, 1966, p. 181). Reading observations of mystics about psychoanalysis, and of psychoanalysts about mysticism, one cannot escape the conclusion that both are fueled by considerable ignorance about the other.

Perhaps the most fundamental difference between psychoanalysis and mysticism lies in their understanding of what constitutes consciousness. Psychoanalysis subscribes to the current scientific consensus, driven by developments in neurosciences, that sees consciousness as an epiphenomenon of brain processes, so that with brain death all consciousness is forever extinguished. In the mainstream of mystical thought is the idea of a personal consciousness being part of a "universal" consciousness from which individual consciousness emerges at birth and into which it ultimately dissolves at death. In more modern language, one would say that for mystics the brain is but a filter, through which the "universal consciousness," or "cosmic self," filters in space–time to form individual, personal selves. In the mystical model, my individual consciousness is not an emergent fragile property of brain processes, as conventional neurosciences would have it, but exists independently of the brain that has filtered it through neurological, cognitive, cultural, and social processes. Consciousness does not originate in the brain which is but a filter. Mystics (as also some artists), it is believed, can bypass this filter and tap into the universal consciousness.

Even if the two models of consciousness are irreconcilable, are there ways in which psychoanalysts and mystic gurus are siblings and can perhaps learn from each other? My answer is a qualified "yes." Let me begin with the healing aspect of the interaction between the guru and the seeker in the Indian traditions and the contribution this understanding, including the self-understanding of the traditions, can make to psychoanalysis.

The healing interaction in spiritual traditions and in psychoanalysis

In theory, Indian spiritual traditions generally view their healing function, both of mind and body, as incidental to and as a by-product of their main task: the purification of the mind, the removal of its distortions and illusions—its ignorance, in Buddhist terms. A purified mind is calm (or mindful) and thus a fit receptacle for the flow of a higher, transcendent consciousness. In most forms of Yoga, for instance, the body, though important, is considered as subordinated to the mind. The gross body, our material sheath, is viewed as a shadow or creation of the subtle body we call the mind. The body is a mold into which the mind pours itself, a mold that has been prepared and can be changed by the mind (Sri Aurobindo, 1911). Impurities of the mind not only lead to mental distress and illness but also, physically translated, manifest themselves in the body as disease. The removal of the cause—the impurities—also means the cessation of the effect: distress and disease.

A purified mind makes for a pure body, a perfected mind for the perfection of the body. The perfection of the body, however, is not simultaneous with that of the mind but delayed till the impure precipitates of the mind, including karmic traces from past lives, have worked themselves out. This is a process which should not disturb the spiritual seeker although some may attempt to accelerate the purification of the body by certain forms of Yoga, such as the Hathayoga. Moreover, the spiritual disciplines are believed to be accompanied by profound alterations in brain physiology and chemistry, in the nervous system, in the digestive and secretive processes. These cannot be effected without some physical disturbances which, though, are temporary and never more than are necessary for the process.

In practice, of course, for most people, the attraction of a spiritual discipline, especially if a famous spiritual guide teaches it—the guru, rinpoche, roshi, pir, or any other kind of teacher—lies more in an expectation of immediate healing by the teacher than in an indeterminate promise of a purified mind and eventual spiritual perfection through meditation. Although there is a large variety of Eastern meditative practices, the differences between them perhaps insufficiently appreciated in psychoanalytic literature (Epstein, 1990), there is a much greater uniformity in the way the spiritual teacher is regarded across the Eastern traditions. The complete devotion and unquestioning faith expected of the seeker by the Hindu guru, for instance, is identical with the expectations entertained by the Tibetan Buddhist master, in spite of the differences in their respective Yogic and Tantric meditation practices. In other words, the teacher more than the meditative discipline incorporates a therapeutic potential which draws to him many seeking relief from emotional distress or physical suffering. This is certainly true of the devotees of well-known Indian gurus I have studied over the years (Kakar, 1982, 1991).

The prominence of the healing offer is especially marked in case of some gurus like the late Sathya Sai Baba, with a worldwide following numbering in tens of millions, who may fairly be described as the healer guru *par excellence*. An unusually large number of stories told about him by devotees are narratives of "miraculous" healing. To a lesser extent, this is also true about spiritual guides whose healing offer is less conspicuous. In a study of Ma Anandamayi ("Mother of Bliss"), a famous female guru of north India with a large following, including the former Indian Prime Minister Indira Gandhi, eleven of forty-three interviews with her disciples contained incidents of her healing exploits (Hallstrom, 1999, p. 116). Even in the case of an "intellectual," modern guru like J. Krishnamurti, with a following among the most modern and highly educated sections of society, it is not his teaching but the news about his miraculous cures that excited the greatest interest (Jayakar, 1986, p. 211).

Reading or listening to a number of healing stories, what one learns again and again are, one, accounts of the guru's extraordinary empathy and, two, the devotee's surrender: both empathy and surrender pushed to a point that would cause most analysts considerable unease.

Empathy and spiritual healing

In interviews with seeker–patients, and in reading their accounts, what I have found most striking about the healing encounter in the spiritual traditions is the seeker–patient's conviction of being profoundly understood by the teacher. In case after case, sometimes even in the first encounter, we hear reports of how the teacher saw deep into the patient's heart, looked into the innermost recesses of their being, and of the effect this understanding had on them.

Mahamaya is a middle-aged Bengali woman who first met Sai Baba in 1992 and has remained a devoted follower ever since. She grew up in a middle-class household in Calcutta and remembers that both her parents had strong devotional and spiritual leanings. The outer shell of her biography—the events of her life: education, arranged marriage, children, part-time work as a teacher while her husband climbs the bureaucratic ladder in a state-owned insurance company—follows the conventions of an Indian middle-class success story. There are, however, tantalizing hints of unhappiness in the marriage during its early years, some episodes of depression, especially one following the surgical removal of a malignant tumour in the kidney just before she met Sai Baba. Mahamaya may be sparing in the narration of painful events of her life but not in the description of her emotional state prior to the first meeting with Swami (master).

"I was steeped deep in crisis, and altogether shattered in body and mind. At that stage of my life, I was weak and had physically broken down, mentally in utter darkness. I was groping for true and abiding support" (Agarwal, 2000, p. 7).

Visiting Baba's ashram together with her husband, she is sitting among a number of other visitors when Baba motions the couple to move to a smaller room adjoining the main hall for a private interview. Let me take the story forward in her own words:

> As soon as my eyes met Swami's, he said, "So you have come, with how much love I have called you."
>
> What a moment! A storm raged within me. I was stunned, dazed, and then broke down in a storm of tears. Since 1988, life had been a struggle for me, beset with moments of trouble, mental agony, anguish, and depression overcoming me now and then. But never had I opened my heart to anyone, not even my husband.

> God was the sole companion of my broken heart. An introvert
> from childhood, I had not even opened my heart to my parents.
> Something happened to me the moment I looked into the divine
> eyes. All restraint, and all constraints just vanished, tears welled up
> in my eyes and poured down my cheeks. I was sobbing like a child.
> I felt my heart was purified through and through. (ibid., p. 28)

Baba then tells her that

> I should not worry about my son who, being busy with studies,
> was not writing letters. Secondly, I need not bother about my
> arthritis. In due course the pain would be reduced even though it
> would not go altogether. Thirdly, my younger daughter would have
> a safe delivery. These thoughts were in my mind no doubt but I had
> not uttered a word to him on these matters. He is the indweller.
> He knows all that goes on in our mind. (ibid., pp. 29–30)

Over the years Mahamaya's healing is evident in a marked increase in
her zest for life and a creative outpouring in which she writes many
poems and songs in Bengali and Hindi.

The patient's feeling of being deeply understood by the teacher, of the
Swami being the "indweller"—of the teacher's empathy, the analyst will
say—is a primary feature of the healing discourse in Eastern, especially
Hindu and Tantric Buddhist spiritual traditions. I would suggest here
that an exploration of the basic features of the guru's empathy can
make a significant contribution to the psychoanalytic discussion of
empathy and the ways in which it gets communicated by the analyst
to the patient.

It seems to me that empathy, Freud's *Einfuehlung*, the "feeling into"
another person, has been the object of a good deal of ambivalence in
psychoanalytic literature, an ambivalence that has perhaps to do with what
Freud, in a letter to Ferenczi, called its "mystical character" (Grubrich-
Simitis, 1986, p. 271). The *Oxford English Dictionary*'s definition of
empathy seems unabashedly "mystical" when it defines it as "the power of
projecting one's personality into (and so fully comprehending) the object
of contemplation." Although empathy constitutes the foundation of
psychoanalytic work, of the essence for gathering data for analytic interpretation, its connection to poorly understood unconscious processes in
the analyst and to a required permeability of his self (with the attendant

dread of a loss of self), has surrounded the concept with a degree of unease in psychoanalytic discussion. Its general usage in psychoanalysis as one person's capacity to partake of the inner experience of another through unconscious attunement skims over the underlying mystery of the process. In other words, how does our normal non-empathic state, a state of self experience with thoughts which are usually self related (Satran, 1991), change into a state where we can transcend the boundaries of the self to share the conscious and unconscious feelings and experiences of another self? Even the analyst's psychic state that is conducive to the operation of empathy, namely his evenly suspended, free-floating attention, when examined closely, seems to belong as much (if not more) to the meditative practices of spiritual traditions as to a "scientific" psychoanalysis. Consider, for instance, Freud's (1923a) description of this psychic state:

> Experience soon showed that the attitude which the analytic physician could most advantageously adopt was to surrender himself to his own unconscious mental activity, in a state of evenly suspended attention, to avoid as far as possible reflection and the construction of conscious expectations, not to try to fix anything that he heard particularly in his memory, and by these means catch the drift of the patient's unconscious with his own unconscious. (p. 239)

Ehrenzweig (1964) has called free-floating attention "unconscious scanning" which depends on a conscious blankness and is liable to be disturbed by introspection. Unconscious scanning clearly has a meditative character, very different from the process of introspection. Ehrenzweig compares unconscious scanning to Paul Klee's "multidimensional attention" or to "horizontal listening" in music where one hears polyphonic voices, as opposed to normal, "vertical" listening where one follows a single melody underscored by a harmonic background of accompanying voices. Horizontal hearing, in which several voices contending for exclusive attention cancel each other out, is totally blank in so far as conscious memory is concerned. This conscious blankness, however, does not preclude precision and fullness of information. In such comparisons and descriptions of (an ideal) free-floating attention (Bion, 1967; Eyre, 1978), expert meditators will not fail to recognize advanced stages of meditative contemplation in certain Hindu and Buddhist spiritual disciplines, such as the *shamatha* practice of sitting meditation without object or goal. In other words, the analyst's potential for unconscious scanning or what Ogden (1997) calls the use of reverie experience, namely his unobtrusive thoughts, feelings, fantasies, ruminations, daydreams, bodily sensations, and so on, seemingly unconnected to what the patient is saying at the moment, may well be related to his capacity for metaphysical openness. It is this openness which bears on his capacity "to feel the alive moments of an analytic session in a visceral way, to be able to hear that a word or a phrase has been used, has been made anew in an interesting, unexpected way" (Ogden, 1997, p. 719).

The increasing psychoanalytic ambivalence toward empathy seems to have its origins in (how could it be otherwise?) Freud's changing views towards the phenomenon as he aged. Paul Roazen, in his introduction to a paper by Hélène Deutsch (1989), suggests that Freud took a far more distant and detached view of his patients in his later years than in an earlier, healthier period. Although in 1921, in his draft of "Psychoanalysis and telepathy," the "secret essay" that was published posthumously (1941d), Freud had been sympathetic to the operation of such an "occult" phenomenon as telepathy and thus, presumably, to the non-rational, intuitive, "occult" aspects of empathy, by 1927 he was taking a much more unambivalent stance on behalf of positivist science:

> The riddles of the universe reveal themselves only slowly to our investigation; there are many questions to which science today can give no answer. But scientific work is the only road which can lead us to a knowledge of reality outside ourselves. It is once again merely an illusion to expect anything from intuition and introspection; they can give us nothing but particulars about our own mental life, which are hard to interpret, never any information about the questions which religious doctrine finds it easy to answer. (Freud, 1927c)

All his close followers did not share Freud's criticism of intuition and introspection; Hélène Deutsch (1926), for instance, viewed the analyst's intuition as a powerful therapeutic tool. Yet with hardening attitudes toward the "occult" in the wake of Freud's distancing from it, empathy too became an object of suspicion since there were no satisfactory criteria that distinguished it from telepathy in the analytic situation (Rycroft, 1954).

In contemporary psychoanalysis, the unease with empathy is expressed variously. Many psychoanalytic contributions on the nature of empathy (Levy, 1985) seek to temper its self-transcendental character by emphasizing that the analyst's identification with the patient is transient, non-regressive, and under the analyst's ego control. Beginning with Freud (Grubrich-Simitis, 1986, p. 272; Pigman, 1995), other analysts have emphasized the intellectual and rational aspects of empathy. They have sought to domesticate its highly subjective, experiential character by enlarging the scope of the concept to include more neutral and cognitive aspects. Empathy, they assert, is not only an unconscious process in which the analyst shares the patient's experience for a short time but it also includes the placing of this experience in a larger, more objective, and complex understanding of the patient and then responding with an appropriate interpretation (Levy, 1985). The analyst's unconscious resonance with the patient oscillates with a more intellectual attitude (Reich, 1966), to produce what has been called "generative empathy" (Schaefer, 1959), "vicarious introspection" (Kohut, 1959), or "emotional knowing" (Greenson, 1960).

Yet others, again going back to Freud who pointed out the difficulty of knowing whether our empathy is not merely the projection of our own feelings onto the patient (Freud, 1912–13, p. 103), have surrounded empathy with danger signals (Buie, 1981; Moses, 1988; Shapiro, 1974; Spence, 1988; Tuch, 1997). What we often take for empathy may only be an empathic fantasy (Satran, 1991), a projective distortion (Spence, 1988). Empathy is also imprecise in that the range of empathic immersion into another person can extend from a state of minimal feeling with him to the extreme of nearly becoming the other person and thus psychotic (Satran, 1991, p. 739). A prolonged identification with the patient is quite likely to be a pathological gratification of the analyst's own unconscious needs (Greenson, 1960).

The overwhelming majority of psychoanalytic contributions on the nature of empathy, then, have tried to distance it (perhaps also defensively?) from its moorings in unconscious, still poorly understood, but no longer completely mysterious mental states which, as we shall see later, seem to be quite similar to those traversed during the meditative process. Even Kohut's important contribution does not lie as much in the reclamation of empathy in its "mystical," experiential sense but in his emphasizing it as a primary tool of gathering psychoanalytic data and in raising its status to that of a vital curative agent in psychoanalysis; even incorrect or contradictory interpretations of different analytic schools can be therapeutically effective so long as the analyst's empathic resonance with the patient's psychic state is also being conveyed through other means of communication (Kohut, 1984, pp. 94–95).

Spiritual perspectives, of course, postulate the roots of empathy in a transcendent unconscious that lies in a deeper layer of the mind than the strata in which the biological and life historical unconscious are located. At this deepest level, the transcendent unconscious is said to connect with the hidden order of the universe or, in another formulation, is united with the consciousness animating all existence. In its highest state, this empathy is the common truth both in a human being and in the heart of existence. Since it lies beyond conscious awareness, great artists, writers, and music-makers have often felt that their creative imagination, the product of heightened empathy, comes from outside themselves, that it is not self-centered. Considered almost as a truism in classical Indian aesthetics, this has also been the position of many artists and writers in the West in the premodern era although their modern counterparts are reluctant to openly embrace such a "spiritual" outlook. In his Nobel Prize acceptance speech, the writer Saul Bellow observes:

> The sense of our real powers, powers we seem to derive from the universe itself, also comes and goes … We are reluctant to talk about this because there is nothing we can prove, because our language is inadequate, and because few people are willing to risk talking about it. They would have to say that there is a spirit, and that is taboo. (cited in Knight, 1987, p. 365)

Premodern geniuses, certainly in India, had no such inhibition. Mirza Ghalib, the great nineteenth-century Urdu poet, could write: *Aate hain ghaibse ye/mazamiin khyal mein/ Ghalib sareer e khama/navaye sarosh hai*; "My thoughts come to me / From somewhere beyond / When Ghalib is attuned / To the music of the stars."

Creativity that springs from extraordinary empathy not only repairs the damage in the life of a genius but rips up its limits imposed by instincts and narcissism. Extraordinary artistic creativity is thus neither compensation nor sublimation of deep pain that reaches back into childhood. The pain only serves to open up a channel in the artist for the flow of a power that both creates and cures.

From the spiritual perspective, the analyst's empathy would be seen as the cornerstone of the healing process, and to remove the obstacles to his own empathy, the analyst's primary task of developing as a healer. It is instructive that the words patient and empathy (Greek: *pathein*, Latin: *pati*) have the same roots. In empathy, we go beyond the limits of the self and join, even etymologically, the patient (Mahony, 2012). The analyst's identity would then be more akin to that of the creative artist, writer, or poet than of the doctor. As the English poet John Keats describes the poet's identity (he uses the word "character"):

> As to the poetic Character itself—it is not itself—it has no self—it is everything and nothing. It has no character—it enjoys light and hate; it loves in gusto, be it foul or fair, high or low— it has as much delight in conceiving an Iago as an Imogen. What shocks the virtuous philosopher, delights the chameleon Poet—A Poet is the most unpoetical of anything in existence; because he has no identity—Not one word I ever utter can be taken for granted as an opinion growing out of my identical nature—the identity of everyone begins to press upon me. (Keats, 1958, pp. 386–387)

Gustave Flaubert, while writing *Madame Bovary*, confides to a friend,

> It is a delicious thing to write, to be no longer yourself but to move in an entire universe of your own creating. Today, for instance, as a man and woman, both lover and mistress, I rode into a forest of an autumn afternoon under the yellow leaves, and I was also the horses, the leaves, the wind, the words my people uttered, even the red sun that made them close their love-drowned eyes. (cited in Margulies, 1993, p. 596)

Informed by the spiritual perspective, the analyst's self is not hidden, as in the earlier ideal of the analyst being a blank screen, but would often appear to be absent, transiently replaced by the experience of the patient.

There are no recipes on how an analyst makes the boundaries of his self more permeable, goes from his sense of being a unique individual, that is, indivisible, to being more—at least in the clinical setting—"dividual," that is, divisible (Marriott, 1976), facilitating the flow of empathy. Most analysts would be skeptical of the claim by spiritual adepts, from all cultures, that extended performance of a meditative practice is accompanied by an extraordinary increase in empathic capacity. But for those analysts who are open to the insights of the spiritual perspective, a first step is a persistent awareness that tolerance and compassion are the precursors to empathy, the base camps in the spiritual climb as I have called them. They can also look to spiritual traditions for pointers in their cultivation. For instance, there are many ways of fostering compassion, from a constant and conscious practice of compassion in dealing with others till it becomes an ingrained way of approaching all living beings, through the specialized techniques such as the "compassionate meditation" of the Buddhists, to a serious engagement with the performance of altruistic acts.

Communication of empathy

In psychoanalysis, the analyst's understanding of the patient's inner state is primarily conveyed through a verbalizable and verbalized interpretation. In other words, the analyst's communication of empathy for the patient's inner state is primarily conveyed through words. Other means of communication, employing the aural, visual, tactile, and olfactory senses, have received a limited attention in analytic literature (Jacobs, 1973, 1994, 1995) although analysts have long known that it is these other nonverbal means and not words which constitute the fundamental layer of human communication in infancy (Spitz, 1957). To take the aural sense first, the *music* of healing, the prosodic aspects of the analyst's discourse—tone, accent, pauses, silences, intonation—may amplify, accentuate, or belie the empathy of his words. The importance of prosody differs with individuals but may also vary across cultures. In the major Eastern civilizations, for instance, the formal mode of communication required within the family and especially in hierarchical relationships, the reliance placed on prosody to divine the real meaning of a speaker's words, may be greater than in cultures which hold the "saying what one means" and "meaning what one says" as highly desirable virtues.

The psychoanalytic setting, with the patient lying on the couch and an absence of eye contact between the patient and the analyst during the analytic hour, is actively inimical to the visual aspects—expression in eyes, gestures, facial mimicry, positions of body—of communicating empathy. The psychoanalytic emphasis on free association, fostered through a restriction of the visual channel, outlaws the *dance* of healing even more than its music.

And, of course, because of the rule of abstinence and the dread of "crossing boundaries," amplified by psychoanalytic lore around the transgressions of once heroic and now tragic figures in the history of the discipline (J. M. Ross, 1995), the tactile aspects of empathic communication between the analyst and the patient must perforce be completely excluded. Not for the analyst the clasping of a shoulder, the taking of a hand between one's own, the consoling stroke on the head, which convey empathic connection to a person as nothing else can in his or her periods of acute distress. For the analyst is acutely aware that a touch of understanding can soon become a caress of desire—or a stab of anxiety, a risk that spiritual teachers routinely take, sometimes with disastrous consequences for the disciple.

I must also add that like many people deprived of sight who develop acute aural or tactile perceptions, the emphasis on words in the analytic situation, I believe, increases the patient's (and the analyst's) sensitivity to the nuances and particularities of language. At least this has been my own experience; when in the full throes of transference during my training analysis in Germany, I not only began to dream in German but also to write fiction in that language, a gift that was snatched away when the analysis ended. This enhanced linguistic sensitivity receded when the transferential context which had made it possible disappeared.

Compared to the analyst, then, the spiritual teacher is relatively uninhibited (but also more endangered) in employing the full register of communication to convey his empathic understanding of the patient–seeker's internal state. In describing their experiences of the teacher's empathy, patient–seekers in the Indian traditions often emphasize factors other than the content of his words. "I did not understand but I came away with the words alive within me," is a typical reaction (Jayakar, 1986, p. 8). The Indian traditions even have a technical term for the guru's look, *darshanat*, "through the guru's look," in which the seeker–patient is believed to be seen "in every detail as in a clear mirror" (Swami Muktananda 1983, p. 37).

Like analysts, gurus, too, differ among themselves in their innate empathic capacities. Yet with their meditative practices designed to weaken what Brickman (1998) calls the encapsulation of the self, not in an uncontrolled regression but in controlled decentering experiences, a spiritual discipline seems to open the doors to an empathic responsiveness to the surround, that can extend to the point of a high degree of identification with another person.[10]

Analysts, too, may have these "transcendental" moments during an analytic hour but these do not follow from being a part of a rigorous training explicitly designed to foster the mental state of what Bion called "ignorance" and whose first stage is what Keats (1958) called "negative capability," a passive, receptive state where there is no irritable reaching after fact and reason and no search for meaning. For Keats, it is the "unitive" imagination—an active interchange between mind and its object rather than the impressions the object produces on the mind— which makes the empathic participation in the existence of other persons possible. The poet, perhaps a person of particularly strong empathic development, grasps the "truth" about the animate and inanimate Other through this empathy and then reproduces it in literary images (Leavy, 1970).

In their empathic identifications, analysts can perhaps never go as far as a few gurus are reputed to have done. In describing Anandamayi as a "spiritually realized" person, for instance, a devotee explains:

> It means you have no personal center. The center of the realized person is everywhere. She can identify with whoever comes in contact with her. She becomes yourself and has your problems at the very moment and can help you from inside. (Hallstrom, 1999, p. 98)

---

[10] A radical increase in empathy for another person, claimed by spiritual adepts, is supposedly a part of their generally heightened responsiveness—empathy in its widest sense—toward the animate and inanimate worlds as also is a heightened metaphysical responsiveness.

Another disciple describes her as: "She had no sense of 'I' or 'mine' and often simply mirrored the emotions of those around her; she seemed to have no desires of her own, so the incentives to her behavior took shape out of the wishes of her companions" (p. 26). Here Anandamayi approaches the ideal of the spiritual master met with in almost all the Eastern traditions. In the Sufi tradition, for instance, the Shaykh's

> own bodily form has been annihilated and he has become a mirror; within it are reflected the faces of others … If you see an ugly face, that is you; and if you see Jesus and Mary, that is you. He is neither this nor that, he is plain; he has set your own reflection before you. (Chittick, 1983, p. 145)[11]

The reflecting mirror ideal of the mystical guru, then, is quite different from the earlier psychoanalytic ideal of the analyst as a blank screen; the analyst's self is hidden, unlike that of the guru where it often appears to be absent, transiently replaced by the experience of the Other. Anandamayi, like some gurus, but unlike many analysts, can accompany the patient to the land of pre-psychological chaos met with in psychosis and borderline states. It is perhaps only Bion's (1967) (impossible) ideal analyst who has eschewed memory and desire (and, in a later amendment, has also abandoned understanding), who is a twin of the (also ideal) mystic guru.

Hindu spiritual traditions give detailed descriptions of the process that augments empathy to a point where there is no affective obstacle to an identification with another's experience; the temporal and essential limits to the identification extend to a degree that are inconceivable to our normal consciousness. A complete empathic knowledge of another person, they claim, involves the activation of a normally dormant "higher" faculty or consciousness. In Yogic practice, for instance, reason, imagination, memory, thought, sensations have to first become sufficiently quiet for the higher faculty of Buddhi to become active and to know itself as separate and different from the lower qualities (Sri Aurobindo, 1911). Buddhi is the Yogic analog of Bion's "sense organ" of psychical qualities which responds to the broadcast of a "sender" which dwells in the domain of the inner world,

---

[11] Compare these portraits of the "enlightened" spiritual teacher with Keats' description of the identity—he called it Character—of the poet on p. 116.

quite unlike the three-dimensional space of the external world, to which psychoanalysts need to develop a keener reception. Analysts, Bion maintained, needed to screen out the noise of sensible life—subject it to "a beam of intense darkness," as he poetically put it—so as to become more receptive to other messages from the psychical world (Grotstein, 1981). This receptivity leads to the expansion of preconscious communication channels and a greater capacity for retrieval from the depths of the psyche (Bolognini, 2001).

Surrender

The disciples' accounts of healing encounters with the guru also make it evident that these interactions have the aim of establishing him as highly reliable, always available for what Christopher Bollas (1979) would call a transformational object.[12] The guru furthers this process by his willingness to let the seeker merge with what the latter perceives to be the guru's greatness, strength, calmness, just as the mother once did when she lifted the anxious infant and held him against her body. Sai Baba constantly reminds his devotees that they are not separate from him: "I am in you, outside you, in front of you, above you, below you. I am all the time around you, in your proximity" (Agarwal, 2000, p. 54) and "Anything coming out of the depth of your heart reaches me. So never have any doubt on this account" (ibid., p. 116).

Teachers in many Indian spiritual traditions have always known that a prolonged phase of meditation on the guru's face or form—practised, for instance, in the Guru Yoga of Vajrayana Buddhism or in the Siddha Yoga of Kashmir Shaivism (a Hindu tradition), as also the contemplative uses of the guru's photograph in such modern sects as the Radhasoami Satsang and Sahaja Yoga—will contribute to and hasten the merging experience (Kakar, 1991). As a Siddha Yoga guru, Swami Muktananda (1983), observes: "The mind that always contemplates the guru eventually becomes the guru. Meditation on the guru's form, immerses the meditator in the state of the guru" (p. 3). As I have described elsewhere in a discussion of the Hindu guru as healer (Kakar,

---

[12] Bollas traces the transformational object back to the mother of earliest infancy where she is the total environment of the infant, an object that is identified with the alteration of the infant's self experience.

1991, p. 52), other aspects of the guru–disciple interaction, such as the taking in of *prasada* (food offerings touched or tasted by the guru) or drinking water used to wash his feet, perform a similar function in the loosening of the seeker–patient's self boundaries and an increasing surrender. Gradually, the seeker–patient seems to acquire the capacity of summoning the guru's image with a hallucinatory intensity when in distress. Thus one patient, when lying sick with jaundice, feverish, and in a state of drowsiness, reports: "I do not know if I used to dream or it was reality. I always felt Baba constantly with me. He was caressing me, touching my hands. I never felt lonely. He was there all the time" (Agarwal, 2000, p. 72).

This access to archaic modes of contact in which a hallucinatory image of the guru is created to sustain a self in danger of losing its cohesion is reported by many seeker–patients and seems to be an integral part of the spiritual healing discourse.

With the mystic-guru's focus on serving as a transformational object and providing the seeker–disciple with what Heinz Kohut (1971) calls "a merger with the selfobject"—in contrast to the analyst's effort to consolidate a sense of personal agency—the guru and the context in which he or she functions are intensely engaged in fostering the seeker–patient's idealization of their person. This is because of the signal importance many contemporary, "other-power" spiritual traditions attach to *surrender* as indispensable for mutative changes in the self, a surrender which can be driven forward hugely by intense forces of idealization, an idealization that is actively fostered by the Indian cultural imagination. The guru is essential, not in himself or herself, but as a facilitator for the process in which surrender, *atamsamparn*, takes place. In other words, in contemporary mystical traditions, the guru is an essential conduit, a transitional object to the state of surrender.[13]

As someone believed to be in possession of a higher consciousness, of being in touch with "higher powers," a guru, the "godman," is regarded with awe and reverence in the Indian context. This was not always the

---

[13] Western experience, with demonic charismatic leaders of religious cults or nations (Hitler, Stalin) will naturally have difficulty with the traditional Indian extolling of surrender, of idealization and identification as motors of psychic transformation.

case. In Vedic times (1500–500 BCE) when a human being's encounter with the sacred mysteries took place through ritual, the guru was more a guide to their correct performance and an instructor in religious duties. A teacher deserving of respect and a measure of obedience, he was not yet the mysterious figure of awe and the venerated incarnation of divinity. In the later Upanishadic era (800–500 BCE), the polar shift begins as the person of the guru starts to replace Vedic rituals as the path to spiritual liberation. He now changes from a knower and dweller in Brahman, "ultimate reality," to being the only conduit to Brahman. Yet the Upanishadic guru is still recognizably human, a teacher of acute intellect, astute and compassionate, demanding from the disciple the exercise of his reason rather than exercises in submission and blind surrender. Here, the ideal of the Hindu guru was not too far removed from the Buddhist master who, also, constructed experience-near situations to illustrate a teaching and who saw the master–disciple relationship as one of potential equals with spiritual insight as its goal.

The change from the teacher image of the guru received its greatest momentum with the rise of bhakti cults in both north and south India from the fifth century CE. Devotional surrender on the part of the disciple with such outer features as the worship of the guru's feet, bodily prostration, and other forms of veneration, and divine grace on the part of the guru mark the guru–disciple relationship. The guru is now an extraordinary figure of mystery and power, the godman. "Guru is Brahma, guru is Vishnu, guru is Maheshwara," is a verse familiar to most Hindus.[14]

Surrender of the self is, of course, also to be found in other religious traditions of the world. William James (1902) called it regeneration by relaxing and letting go, psychologically indistinguishable from Lutheran justification by faith and the Wesleyan acceptance of free grace. He characterized it as giving one's private convulsive self a rest and finding that a greater self is there.

"The results, slow or sudden, greater or small, of the combined optimism and expectancy, the regenerative phenomenon which ensues on the abandonment of effort, remain firm facts of human nature" (James, 1902, p. 107).

---

[14] Recall that in the trinity of Hindu gods, Brahma is the Creator, Vishnu, the Preserver, and Maheshwara, another name for Siva, the Destroyer.

He added:

> you see why self-surrender has been and always must be regarded as the vital turning point of religious life. One may say the whole development of Christianity in inwardness has consisted in little more than greater and greater emphasis attached to this crisis of self-surrender. (p. 195)

In Sufism, too, surrender to the master is a necessary prerequisite for the state of *fana fil-shaykh* or annihilation of oneself in the master. Of the *iradah*, the relationship between the Sufi master and his disciple, the Sufi poet says: "O heart, if thou wanted the Beloved to be happy with thee, then thou must do and say what he commands. If he says, 'Weep blood!' do not ask 'Why?'; if He says, 'Die!' do not say 'How is that fitting?'" (Nurbakhsh, 1978, p. 208).

Psychoanalysts generally subscribe to the values of secular humanism and Western individualism in emphasizing personal agency and autonomy, a tradition that equates surrender with submission, defeat (Ghent, 1990). However, there has also been a "minor" line of psycho-analytic thought (Balint, 1979; Kohut, 1977; Winnicott, 1965) extending back to Sándor Ferenczi (1933) in which dependency is not viewed negatively but considered an important constituent of the psyche.[15] Psychoanalytic observations on surrender (e.g., Ghent, 1990; Maroda, 1999; Safran, 2016) have been a natural extension of this line. They have raised questions whether a disregard of the uncontrollable aspects of life and a devaluation of the power of the unconscious in determining the events of one's life promote "an inflated sense of personal agency" and whether this "inflation goes hand in hand with a type of grandiosity that fails to recognize the fundamental otherness or alterity of life" (Safran, 2016, p. 58). The mystical guru's view of surrender brings the "otherness" of life to the forefront. "When you realize that you are not in control of your life, but life is governed by some supreme law, then surrender happens" (Shankar, n.d.).[16] Surrender is also not a process

---

[15] In contrast to the West, *amae*, the desire to depend on the care of authority figures and the expectation of receiving it is encouraged in Japanese child rearing practices (Doi & Schwaber, 2016). This is also true of childrearing in India (Kakar, 1978).

[16] See also Gurudev Sri Sri Ravi Shankar's YouTube videos (2016), *Meaning of Surrender* and *Significance of Surrender* and Sadhguru (2012), *What Is Surrender?*

that is voluntary (Ghent, 1990) but "happens spontaneously with the knowledge that you are not in control of anything—not even your thoughts or feelings" (Shankar, n.d.).

The guru, here a well-regarded contemporary mystic, Gurudev Sri Sri Ravi Shankar will also agree with Bollas and Ghent that surrender is a transformative process in which the self is radically changed, that "Surrender is not an act, it is a state of your being." He will go on to describe the state for his disciples in terms that they can easily comprehend and resonate to:

> When you are grateful for all that you have been given in life, then you are in a state of surrender. When you are totally helpless, and you realize your helplessness, then you are in a state of surrender. Surrender has happened when you know that your life is insignificant in the span of time and space. When you know there are millions and millions of stars, how big the solar system is, where the Earth is—then what is one's life? When you see this, surrender has happened. (Shankar, n.d.)

Another mystic (Muktananda, 1983) describes the experience of surrender in relation to the guru thus:

> When you surrender to the guru, you become like a valley, a vacuum, an abyss, a bottomless pit. You acquire depth, not height. This surrender can be felt in many ways. The guru begins to manifest in you; his energy begins to flow into you. The guru's energy is continuously flowing, but in order to receive it, you have to become a womb, a receptacle. (p. 35)

In his professional work, if not in his life, an Indian analyst who shares a cultural imagination with the mystic-guru would be constantly seeking a balance in the dialectic between the psychoanalytical emphasis on strengthening the sense of personal agency and the process of surrender. Aware of what I have called the "guru fantasy" of his clients that seeks to experience him or her as a guru rather than a doctor and pushes toward surrender, the Indian analyst needs to be conscious that the process of surrender can also immeasurably enhance the receptivity of the patient in the analytic situation, of what is being received from the analyst.

Can the guru learn from the analyst?

Devotees come to the guru, as do patients to the analyst, in a conflicted state. On the one hand, there is the unconscious hope of making up for missing or deficient parental responses of early childhood in interaction with the guru. On the other hand, there is the fear of evoking self-fragmenting responses through the same interaction. The omnipresence of fears of injury to the self and of regression into early primitive states of self-dissolution is what forces the devotees to be wary of intimacy. It prevents the desired surrender to the guru however high the conscious idealization of the values of surrender and letting go might be. Gurus are, of course, aware of the conflict and in their various ways have sought to reassure the disciples about their fears. Muktananda (1983), for instance, writes,

> There are only two ways to life: One is with constant conflict, and the other is with surrender. Conflict leads to anguish and suffering. But when someone surrenders with understanding and equanimity, his house, body and heart becomes full. His former feeling of emptiness and lack disappears. (p. 35)

Gurus are generally aware of the dangers of self-fragmentation and the disciple's defenses against the dreaded inner state. Modern gurus talk explicitly about the agitation and anxiety a disciple may feel when he is close to the guru. The training required en route to surrender is hard and painful. They are aware of the resistances and the negative transferences, the times when the devotee loses faith in the guru, and doubts and suspicions tend to creep in. Do not break the relationship when this is happening, is the general (and analytically sound) advice. The development of inimical feelings toward the guru is part of the process of healing transformation. What is important about the feelings toward the guru is their strength, not their direction. Whether devoted or hostile, as long as the disciple remains turned toward the guru, he will be met by total acceptance. The "ambience of affective acceptance" provided by the guru and his establishment, the *ashram*, will, the master knows, make the disciple feel increasingly safe, shifting the inner balance between need and fear toward the former.

The greater focus on the guru in the spiritual healing interaction, as compared to the analyst–patient relationship, has another consequence: self and guru representations during the course of the transference that are different from those found in the analytic situation. Analysts are, of course, aware that the idealizing transference gives the patient a double vision, both in relation to himself and to the analyst. Within the transference he "sees" the analyst as a parental representation, in the real relationship as a helpful doctor. The two images, in flux over time, constantly condition each other. Because of the co-presence of the patient's adult self, the illusion in relation to the analyst, though it waxes and wanes, remains more or less moderate (Moeller, 1977).

In the spiritual healing relationship, the identity between the actual and the infantile selves of the patient–seeker on the one hand and the real and parental representations of the guru on the other overlap to a much greater extent and for longer periods of time than in psychoanalysis. The double vision in relation to both self and guru representations tends to become monocular, leading to an intensity of idealizing transference that is rarely approached in the psychoanalysis of patients functioning at neurotic levels. In other words, the guru–seeker interaction can touch deeper, more regressed layers of the psyche than is normally the case in psychoanalysis.

From the psychoanalytic viewpoint, gurus need to be aware that even the most powerful and transformative spiritual experiences do not completely rearrange the psychic furniture. A self that has been developing since birth and is, so to speak, physiologically embedded deep in the neuronal networks of the brain, cannot be wiped out by even the most powerful mystical experience. The latter may create new neuronal pathways without, however, erasing the old ones. In times of personal crisis, brought on by great psychological stress or serious illness in old age, there may be an automatic regression to the earlier self as its cut-off parts or unresolved psychic conflicts once again demand a hearing. This is a possibility to which neither the guru nor the disciple is immune. It is especially at these times that mystical traditions need to welcome psychoanalysis which, more than any other psychotherapy, shares their quest for the growth of wisdom and the realization of a higher self. It can thus be helpful to the guru to familiarize him- or herself with the various disguises of desire psychoanalysis has uncovered, including the ones in our dreams.

Where psychoanalysis can contribute most to mysticism is by throwing light on some of the psychological threats faced by gurus which they need to negotiate in their own lives before they can helpfully guide their disciples. There are many gurus who are unaware of the psychological danger posed by the massive idealization of their person by the disciples, a danger that increases exponentially with the number of one's followers and one's prominence as a guru.

Negative feelings, and malignant projections of others toward one's self are easier to handle. They cause severe psychological discomfort, compelling us to reject them by discriminating inside between what belongs to us and what other people are projecting onto us. This painful motivation for repelling the invasion of the self by others does not exist when such projections are very gratifying to our narcissism, our self-esteem, as they invariably are in the case of adoring followers. Who doesn't like to hear, "How great you are, how wonderful, how loving, how wise, you are!" It is difficult to at least not smell the incense smoke being burnt at your altar by so many proclaiming your greatness. A retreat into a feeling of omnipotent grandiosity, while in the sexual sphere a retreat into sexual perversion and predation, has been reported often enough to constitute a specific danger of the guru role. It is sad to hear or read reliable reports about aged gurus who become peeping toms as they arrange, with all the cunning of a voyeur, to spy on their teenaged female disciples (generally Western) undressing for the night in the ashram. The promiscuity of some other gurus, pathetically effortful in the case of elderly bodies with a tendency to flag, is also too well known to merit further repetition.

Conclusion

In conclusion, in spite of being strangers in the divergences of their goals, visions of reality, and views of the self, the psychoanalyst and the guru are siblings in their healing of human suffering and can indeed profitably learn from each other.

This is not to suggest that psychoanalysis should lose its distinctive character by an indiscriminate borrowing from Indian mystical traditions.

For one, psychoanalysis may also be viewed as a singularly modern meditative praxis, unique in its emphasis on being a meditation that is joint rather than individual. Yet in the spirit of Freud's legacy of openness to other disciplines (Freud recommended the study of anthropology, folklore, and mythology to the budding analyst), analysts need to remain open to the possibility that, for instance, an Eastern meditative discipline could become a part of their training if, as claimed by its practitioners, it demonstrably contributes to an enhancement in empathic capability. Indeed, as Clement (2005) has observed, the analyst who has experienced even a short course of meditation is likely to listen to her patient differently. She is likely to be more attuned to subtle, emerging twinges of fear, sadness, or helplessness. Such an analyst is also able to hold these feelings longer and more deeply, without reaching for the reassuring effort to organize and interpret (p. 141).

The traditional Freudian suspicion of the spiritual domain, and the cultural pride in psychoanalysis as a uniquely valuable product of Western civilization and imagination, should not come in the way of such borrowings.

CHAPTER 4

Psyche and nature: Notes from the Indian terroir

Embracing the scientific rationalism of the European Enlightenment, psychoanalysis also adopted the Enlightenment's dominant narrative of the relation between human beings and nature. This narrative was one of human struggle against an implacable enemy and the coming victory due to scientific and technological advances arising from human ingenuity. It was thus dismissive of the European Romantic movement that arose in the late eighteenth century as a protest against a rampant industrialization that was experienced by many as a blight on human habitats. Expressed in poetry, music, and painting, that saw nature as a source of beauty, innocence, and solace to humankind, the Romantic movement was seen by thinkers who had wholeheartedly embraced the philosophy and promise of the Enlightenment as a reactionary response to rationalism.

Freud shared the Enlightenment view of the human struggle against mighty and hostile forces of nature (Devès, 2018) but not the optimistic conclusion of a coming victory that would contribute to human happiness: "With these forces nature rises up against us, majestic, cruel, and inexorable; she brings to our mind once more our weakness and helplessness, which we thought to escape through the work of civilization" (Freud, 1927c, p. 16). Of course, the repressed romantic vision never disappeared but bubbled up from time to time, even in Freud. As Alfredo Lombardozzi (2021) reminds us, Freud in his personal letters and in the paper "On transience" (Freud, 1916a) displays a strongly aesthetic sensibility toward "a nature and an environment which … becomes a sort of travelling companion in the search for a more reflective and perhaps consoling intimacy" (p. 62).

On a conscious level, though, with this dualism in its DNA in which a human being was viewed as wholly separate from his nonhuman environment, the relation of the human psyche to nature remained under the radar of psychoanalytic discourse for almost a century. A notable exception was Harold Searles (1960), who in his book *The Nonhuman Environment in Normal Development and in Schizophrenia* claimed that an ecologically healthy relationship to nature was essential to being human.[17] He averred the infant's subjective oneness with the nonhuman environment and discussed the functions this environment fulfils in various stages of healthy ego development, as also the distortions in this relationship that are uncovered in mental illness.

It is only in the last three decades that nature promisingly entered the ken of psychoanalysis as the ecological crisis took hold and the destructive consequences of climate change became an issue of global concern. Although its impact was circumscribed, the 1992 conference on "Ecological Madness" at the Freud Museum in London (Ward, 1993) was one of the first signs of this expansion of traditional psychoanalytical concerns. As the predictions on the consequences of climate change became more and more dire, there was a palpable increase in psychoanalytic engagement with the deteriorating state of the natural world in professional journals (Lertzman, 2010; Mishan, 1996) and edited volumes (Weintrobe, 2013), a trend that was acknowledged by the International Psychoanalytical Association when in its 2015 meeting in Boston it declared that the IPA needed to increase the widespread consciousness of the precarious state of the natural world due to the activities of humans and that it should promote psychoanalytical

---

[17] Outside psychoanalysis, Bateson (1972) championed the view that human survival would depend upon a way of thinking that stressed not opposition but synergy between the individual and the environment.

research devoted to understanding human interactions with the natural world. Psychoanalytical papers on the environmental crisis (e.g., Devès, 2018; Schinaia, 2019), on unconscious determinants of the denial and disavowal of climate change (Weintrobe, 2013), issues of grief and loss arising from environmental destruction (Randall, 2009), the links between greed, consumption, and climate change (e.g., Weintrobe, 2009) are some of the many papers published in recent years that address the ecological crisis (e.g., Bellamy, 2019; Danil, 2020; Lertzman, 2010; Trapp, 2021.

View from the Indian terroir

The term, terroir, "a sense of place," when used in conjunction with wine (Nossiter, 2009) is a felicitous one for an exploration of the cultural landscape of psychoanalysis. Terroir is a specific place with its soil, climate, and elevation where the wine is made and thus different terroirs, although made with the same sort of grape, produce different wines. The terroir of human beings—historical, geographic, cultural, social, political, religious—too, varies and will produce different psychoanalytic wines. The terroir of psychoanalysis for more than a century has been and continues to be Western, with its distinctive cultural imagination that underlies fundamental ideas about central human experiences. The intimate connection of psychoanalytic thought with Western cultural imagination has remained a relatively unexplored territory in psychoanalytic discourse. The possibility of non-Western cultural imaginations making valuable contributions to the evolution of psychoanalytic thought has not yet been seriously entertained.

As observed earlier, much of this indifference can be attributed to colonialism and its lingering effects (Anderson et al., 2012; Gardner, 1999; Khanna, 2003). How would an Indian vigneron contribute to the understanding of psyche and nature from the Indian terroir?

He would begin by questioning the dualism between the person and his nonhuman environment that seems to have played a critical role in psychoanalytic understanding from the Western terroir. He would wonder if this dualism is not partly due to the Western cultural imagination of the body, sharply differentiated from its surround, a fortress with a limited number of drawbridges connecting it to a hostile surround. In the Indian cultural imagination, on the other hand, the connection between the body and its surround is much more intimate. As discussed elsewhere (Kakar, 1982), the Hindu medical system of Ayurveda imagines a much more open body in intimate and unremitting exchange with its environment, simultaneously accompanied by a ceaseless change within the body. The Indian vigneron would point out that this is also true of traditional art and classical literature.

In contemporary Western literature it is solely the desires and anxieties of the human protagonists that are explored in exquisite detail while the attention given to the nonhuman context in which they live their lives often appears to be perfunctory. Rabindranath Tagore, the Nobel laureate for literature in 1913, highlights the difference between Western and classical Indian literature in his remarks on Shakespeare, whom he greatly admired, and the poetry of fourth-century Sanskrit poet Kalidasa, whom he revered (Tagore, 1922):

> The fury of passion in two of Shakespeare's youthful poems is exhibited in conspicuous isolation. It is snatched away, naked, from the context of the All; it has not the green earth or the blue sky around it; it is there ready to bring to our view the raging fever which is in man's desires, and not the balm of health and repose which encircles it in the universe. (p. 51)

Tagore's (n.d.) eloquent advocacy of the Indian view of nature as essential to the fulfilment of human life[18] is also a plea for balance in the two cultural imaginations and the possibilities for each to enrich the other. What he objected to was the disproportional space Western ideas and its worldview occupied in the modern Indian mind, and thus killed or hampered the opportunity to create a new combination of truths. In the current intellectual domination of Western systems of knowledge, the danger to Indian cultural imagination of a person's relationship to the nonhuman environment is much more immediate. Modern Indians are in the process of losing the pivot of this relationship: sympathy, the

---

[18] It is important to reiterate that I am speaking of cultural imagination of the forest and not the actual Indian forest that is undergoing many depredations and is the site of struggles for the rights of indigenous forest-dwelling tribes.

feeling of kinship that extends beyond what is our kin, a sense of "we" that extends beyond kinship into the nonhuman environment.

> When we know this world as alien to us, then its mechanical aspect takes prominence in our mind; and then we set up our machines and our methods to deal with it and make as much profit as our knowledge of its mechanism allows us to do so," Tagore writes. "This view of things does not play us false … this aspect of truth cannot be ignored; it has to be known and mastered. Europe has done so and reaped a rich harvest … For us the highest purpose of this world is not merely living in it, knowing it and making use of it, but realizing our own selves in it through expansion of our sympathy; not alienating ourselves from it and dominating it, but comprehending and uniting it with ourselves in perfect union. (Tagore, n.d.)

Such a fate, the loss of sympathy, may not be looked at with equanimity. In a globalized world that links not only entertainment and capital flows but also ideas, the bankruptcy of the East will also have an impact on the Western mind, make it poorer. To adapt Tagore's words, if the great light of culture becomes extinct in the East, the horizon in the West will mourn in darkness.

With the Indian cultural imagination as his backdrop, the Indian vigneron would suggest an expansion of the psychoanalytic model of the person. Psychoanalysis conceives of the person essentially as part of her bodily, psychic, and social, interpersonal orders. Mental representations of bodily drives and processes and of experiences with one's social groups, beginning with the family, and the interactions between the two as the person develops through the life cycle, constitute the core constituents of the psyche. From the Indian perspective, though, a person is also a part of his cosmic order. The cosmos, as I visualize it, has two aspects, one subtle and the other, well, earthly, nature. The subtle aspect of the cosmos is the "spiritual" order which has been variously conceptualized by different cultures at various times of history as animated by gods, ancestral spirits, demonic beings or, in more sophisticated formulations, as God, Universal Spirit, or simply the Sacred. Excepting the Jungians, the spiritual aspect of the cosmos is alien to the sensibility of most Freudian analysts, even evoking a reflective antipathy in some, and I will confine myself to the material, earthly aspect of the cosmos—our nonhuman environment.

The earthly aspect of the cosmos is the environment—nature of terrain, quality of air, sunlight, birds, animals, trees and flowers, seasons and so on—in which we are born and live our lives. The neglect of the cosmos, in its spiritual and especially its nonhuman dimension in the development of the psyche, the Indian vigneron would claim, comes from a modern Western orientation that limits a person to being a soma, psyche, and polis, existing in the somatic, psychic, and social orders, but excludes the vital dimension of cosmic order. As an aside, I wonder whether the cosmos would have played a greater role in psychoanalytic theorizing if the setting of psychoanalytic therapy had not been a closed room, suitable for the European climate, but took place out in the open, under a banyan tree that figures so prominently as the preferred setting of the guru–seeker interaction in the Indian traditions.

The significance of nature, the earthly aspect of the cosmos for the psychic well-being can be best understood by reflecting upon the state of loneliness, which the poet Emily Dickinson (1861) evokes in the lines, "the Horror not to be surveyed / But skirted in the Dark / With Consciousness suspended." Loneliness, which assumed a signal importance during the pandemic, feels like a drying out of what I would call the "erotic field," the land of life-giving and life-promoting forces, in which we otherwise live our lives.

When I say that loneliness is a drying out of the erotic field, I mean loneliness is a depletion of loving connectedness, a seepage of the life force which, at its extreme, is equated with dying and death. The erotic field itself consists of the person's myriad connections to the not-self, both in the inner and outer worlds. We normally equate the not-self with human "Others," including the mental representations in the psyche of loved ones who are no longer alive. Indeed, stable mental representations of loving connectedness within the family while growing up are some of the more vital parts of the erotic field. Yet, there are many other connections to the earthly aspect of the cosmos, to nature, that we barely register and become aware of them only when the connection is lost.

A patient who had long waited to migrate to the United States had his wish fulfilled when he got a well-paying job in New York. In spite of a great improvement in his material living conditions he soon discovered how unhappy the move had made him. It was not only his family and friends that he missed but the familiar faces he encountered every day on his way to work in Delhi: the sidewalk barber shaving a customer who would nod to him, the recognition in the eyes of the vegetable vendor he passed by, the smile of a child on her way to school, a child he did not personally know. The recognition connecting them was a part of his erotic field as much as the flowers in the neighbor's garden or the roadside tree with a roughly hewn stone idol of Vishnu leaning against the base of its trunk, marigold petals strewn on and around the idol by passing devotees, where he stopped each morning for a quick bow with his raised hands pressed together in genuflection before continuing on his way to work.

Loneliness is not solitude which some people eagerly seek and which many creative people fervently embrace. Most people fear solitude, confusing it with loneliness and its associated absences and silences, and seek to avoid being alone by fretfully seeking the company of other people or, in their absence, by hours of internet surfing or television watching. As Kierkegaard (1844) has put it, "one does everything possible by way of diversions and the Janissary music of loud-voiced enterprises to keep lonely thoughts away" (p. 107). Solitude is not seclusion, its absence of other people in no way a reflection of an inner emptiness but of a fullness, its silence resounding with myriad voices. In solitude, the self is wealthy; in loneliness, destitute.

The difference between loneliness and solitude thus does not solely lie in the fact that the latter is freely chosen whereas loneliness invariably feels imposed. The critical difference lies in the fact that unlike in loneliness, the erotic field in solitude is reconfigured and not depleted. Memories of loving connectedness with others, especially the early ones with all their intensity, become more plentiful and come to the fore in the inner world while the nonhuman connections in the outer world assume a salience that was earlier ignored or denied to them. Indeed, in some creative persons, a reconnection, nay, a re-immersion in the earthly cosmos of nature, is not only an antidote to loneliness but is experienced as an elevated feeling of aliveness. The American poet-philosopher, Henry David Thoreau, in his solitary forest retreat would write that his daily dip in the Walden Pond reminded him of nature's endless capacity to renew life and stir him to higher aspirations.

Whenever the Indian poet-philosopher Rabindranath Tagore felt lonely and depressed, "stranded in a desolation where every individual has to struggle through his own problems unaided" (Tagore, 1913), he would withdraw into remote countryside and wall himself off from any but the most perfunctory human contact. In a reconfiguring of the erotic field, the connection with his surround, the natural environment assumed an unparalleled awareness:

> My feelings seem to be those of our ancient earth in the daily ecstasy of its sun-kissed life; my own unconscious seems to stream through each blade of grass, each sucking root, to rise with the sap through the trees, to break out with joyous thrills in the waving fields of corn, in the rustling palm leaves. I feel impelled to give expression to my blood tie with the earth, my kinsman's love for her, but I am afraid I shall not be understood. (Tagore, 1921, p. 40)

Loneliness foreshadows death in that the drying out of the erotic field in loneliness portends its obliteration in death. Losing its fertility in loneliness, the erotic field turns into an unearthly Martian desert in dying. The "nightmare" of dying and death in modern consciousness does not lie in the fears associated with an afterlife but on death stripping the self of all connections, of memories of which the most vital are of persons we have loved and who have loved us but also of the surround in which these memories are located and of which we are much less aware. In psychoanalytic language, the dread lies in the self being emptied of the mental representations of our most important attachment figures and of experiences in our earthly cosmos.

The obliteration of attachments, the erotic field turning into a dust bowl, are vividly conveyed in *Prantik* (Tagore, 1938), a cycle of eighteen poems on dying, death, and "afterdeath," which Tagore wrote in September 1937 after he recovered from an illness which had sent him into a coma for sixty hours. These poems are an exemplary illustration of Tolstoy's observation that the function of art is to make that understood which in the form of argument would be incomprehensible: in this case, the close association of dying with the drying out of the erotic field of which nature is a part. In poem 14 of *Prantik*, for instance, the imagery of dying is almost solely from the natural world.

> It's time for the bird to depart.
> The nest will be empty.
> In the strong winds of the forest, shorn of songs,
> the vacant nest will drop in dust,
> along with the dry leaves and the wilted flowers.
> Day and night will I fly in the trackless space,
> beyond the sunset sea. (p. 53)

The restoration of the self, the greening of the erotic field through a connect with nature is not just an affectation of some nineteenth-century romantic writers. The restorative connect to nature can range from a mild to intense feeling of relatedness which, at the extreme, as in the Tagore quote above, can be experienced as a fusion. Indeed, it has been suggested (Kassouf, 2017) that the intense feelings of relatedness to nature may be essential to the creative process.

Implications for psychoanalysis

It is important to reiterate that the suggested addition of the cosmos to the soma-psyche-polis model of the person does not alter the traditional analytic model but merely expands it. Bringing nature, "earthly cosmos," into the model, highlights the person's embeddedness in his nonhuman environment and thus fosters the widening of the person's connective, empathetic capacities. It strengthens the view that psychoanalysis is not just a medical treatment but also a transforming quest for self-knowledge that extends the analysand's range of compassion and empathy—the beginnings of true wisdom.

A second implication for psychoanalysis in engaging with the view of nature from the Indian terroir could be a reassessment of long-established ideas on the nature of the unconscious id. I have elaborated on this in an earlier chapter. As discussed there, it is the forest that exemplifies the idea of nature in the Indian cultural imagination. The Indian vision of the nature and thus of an unconscious id is of an essentially benign entity that nourishes human concerns and is indispensable in realizing the purpose of human life.

Such a reassessment will not only subscribe to the classical psychoanalytic view of the dynamic unconscious as a repository of repressions and deprivations but also conceive it as a fount of the healing Eros. Eros, like desire, is a concept difficult to pin down, with sexuality at one pole of its continuum and the life preservation instinct or life energy at the other, with many shades of desire and love along the way. It is the life giving and life sustaining force that is the source of an intense feeling of being alive, of spontaneity, creativity, and especially *connectivity* to both our human and nonhuman environment. When Freud writes that the power of the id expresses the true purpose of the individual organism's life and this consists in the satisfaction of its innate needs, then the flow of Eros could be highlighted as an innate need of the unconscious, the analytic process removing the blockages and inhibitions, accumulated over the life cycle and especially during early childhood, to the flow of Eros.

CHAPTER 5

Desire in old age

We are all fated to grow old (excepting those who will meet untimely deaths), yet it is a fate that is rarely fully admitted to our conscious awareness. We do not allow the piercing and cold realization that one will become an old man or woman to strike home emotionally. That one will become a colorless husk without the luster and shine of youth, even as we spend substantial time and energy, at least from middle age onwards, in trying to avert our common fate.

Even as others see us changing from outside, we continue to see ourselves from inside, reluctantly and glacially slow in revising our inner image to match the one reflected by the mirror. And in our innermost self, even that slow adjustment is declined.

Freud hints at his own denial of old age, and a sudden sharp and cruel breach in this defense, in a footnote to his essay on "The 'uncanny'," published when he was sixty-three (Freud, 1919h). Travelling in a train by night, there is a violent jolt that swings back the door of the adjoining washing-cabinet, and an elderly gentleman in a dressing gown and a traveling cap steps into Freud's compartment. To his dismay, the old man, whose appearance Freud thoroughly dislikes, turns out to be his own reflection in the mirror of the washing-cabinet, visible through the open door (p. 243). Contrary to Freud's interpretation wherein he attributes his dislike of his reflection to the vestigial trace of a reaction to an uncanny "double," Stephen Frosch (2013) convincingly argues that the mirror image of the old man is a dismaying presence from the future, rather than from the past, that haunts Freud's present. Freud's angry exclamation to a young female analysand, H.D., "I am an old man. You do not think it worthwhile to love me" (Doolittle, 1956) is further taken as a sign of his distaste for an aging self.

Leaving aside the question whether Freud's (1905a) view that the mental processes of people older than fifty are inelastic and thus they are unsuitable for psychoanalytic treatment has its antecedents in Freud's own personal stance toward old age, it is fortunate that a number of analysts did not make Freud's reservations their own. In an exhaustive review of psychoanalytic literature of the last hundred years on the psychoanalysis of the elderly, Plotkin (2014) shows that a number of analysts have not only refuted Freud's claim of old-age rigidity but, in some cases (e.g., Cohen, 2005; Coltart, 1991; King, 1980; Pollock, 1982), turned it on its head, finding older adults more insightful, focused, and less defensive. Yet, it is also true that, by and large, psychoanalysts still hesitate to take older patients into therapy and that the analytic literature is parsimonious as far as older patients are concerned (Junkers, 2006; Plotkin, 2014, p. 35). Freud's pessimism continues to haunt psychoanalysis in spite of the demographic changes all over the world, meaning, with the increase in life expectancy, the potential clientele for analytic therapy would be increasingly old.

Over time, the reason for the paucity of old people in psychoanalytic therapy has shifted in focus from the older patient to the countertransference problems of the therapist, especially of the analyst who is considerably younger than the aged analysand (Hinze, 1987; King, 1980, p. 159; Wagner, 2005; Wylie & Wylie, 1987).

This is not to deny the existence of some real issues in the analysis of an old person when the therapist is younger. To empathize with a patient in a stage of life which one has to still traverse oneself is a difficult task. The countertransference problems of the analyst, however, have their source not only in the stage of the analyst's life cycle or in his individual life history but also in the narratives around aging of the culture in which he has been socialized. The attitudes of the therapist's cultural group toward the old person, whether of idealization, denigration, or generally in some combination of the two, can be a stubborn part of his countertransference reactions, preventing him from seeing the face behind the mask of an old person clearly.

In my own society, India, as in many other traditional societies, the old person is still largely idealized as a potential repository of wisdom and a model for a longed-for spiritual serenity. I do not mean to imply that this idealization is absent in modern Western societies. In fact, it can enter even the most sensitive analyst's theorizing on old age. In Erik Erikson's (1950) influential eight stages of the human life cycle, formulated when he was around fifty years old, the crisis of old age is portrayed as one of integrity versus despair, with the old person, if all has gone well, emerging with the "virtue" of wisdom. The "wise old man" is a construction that Erikson (1987) in his eighties and now himself a citizen of the republic of old age, disavowed as too simplistic.

In most cultures, the idealization of old age is not without some denigration that, in the case of the old man, condescendingly pities his physical and mental decline. In contrast to some modern societies in which old age is rapidly losing any luster it might have once had, in India an old man still commands a modicum of respect. He may be derisively called a *buddhau*, in other words a gaffer, an old geezer, but never "an old fart." In part, the denigration of the old, and this would be common to both the sexes, may rest on a collective unconscious fantasy that old age represents a piling-up of undischarged remnants of a lifetime of eating and drinking, and is thus dirtier than youth. Growing old means to grow dirty (Kubie, 1937).

The denigration of old women is even less kindly. As a *buddhia*, she carries not only a taint of mental deficiency but more sinisterly, the old woman also touches a layer of collective horror associated with stories of village crones who turn out to be witches.

If cultural narratives of old age impinge on the therapist's counter-transference reactions, the onslaught is even more insidious in the narratives of an old person's sexuality, which is uniformly viewed with distaste, if not worse ... across all cultures. Sexual life, it seems, is the province of youth, an attitude that is also not foreign to many analysts. More than thirty years later, Nancy Miller's observation, based on a review of research findings, that, "With the exception of a few isolated examples, the psychoanalytic literature on aging omits sustained emphasis on sexuality (Cath & Miller, 1986, pp. 174–175), still holds true.[19] And across cultures, evidence of sexual desire in the older man is laughable at best; "*Buddhe ko jawaani chadhi*"—"old geezer playing the young man," is a common taunt in north India. It seems the only role left for an old man is to play the good-natured, slightly foolish grandfather. The remotely sexual encounters he can have with women, if he is lucky, are (in words of the ninety-year-old hero of a 2006 novel by Gabriel García Marquez), "the provocations our young female friends permit themselves because they think we are out of commission" (p. 44).

Sexuality is nonexistent in the old woman to the point that even an attempt by an aging woman to look attractive is met with opprobrium—"*Buddhi ghodi, lal lagaam*"—or, "old mare, red reins," a familiar saying in north India. Sexuality in the older female becomes disgusting to the extent of inviting punitive action if, contrary to all norms of decency, it is ever manifested.[20] The fate of Shurpnakha in the revered Indian epic, Ramayana, is a salutary reminder. Much older than the epic's hero, the youth Rama—Valmiki's Sanskrit version describes her as having thinned brown hair, while in Kamban's Tamil version of the Ramayana she is at least middle-aged and would have appeared as "old" and "haggardly" to the prince—Shurpnakha has the presumption to frankly proposition Rama. Spurned by him, he mockingly passes her on to his brother Lakshmana where she meets a similar rejection. Taunted by both the brothers, she suffers the final indignity of having her nose cut off by Lakshmana, a fantasized clitoridectomy. It is her inconsolable anguish which enflames her brother, the demon king Ravana, to seek revenge and initiates the epic's war between forces of good and evil.

To explore the sexual imagination of the elderly, I have taken recourse to literature and to follow its fictional heroes and heroines as they

---

[19] For an exception see Segal (2013).

[20] Analysts are not immune to the disquiet aroused by the sexuality of an old woman. Wagner (2005) reports of the burst of uneasy laughter that erupts in a group of analytically oriented clinicians when, in a case presentation, Wagner narrates her seventy-nine-year-old female patient's sexual fantasies around her young tennis pro.

navigate the treacherous shoals of old-age sexuality. Given my interest in cultural shaping of the psyche, it is a matter of regret that, although Indian mythology is alive to the problem of old age desire in myths of old sages being seduced by young *apsaras* (the heavenly courtesans), or in legends of kings Puru and Bhishma sacrificing their own sexual lives for the pleasures of their old sires, Indian writers of fiction, with a couple of exceptions, have shunned the subject of aged sexuality. And even in the exceptional cases, the exploration of sexual imagination of the elderly protagonists is hesitant and unsure, the moral universe of the writers inhibiting the full flow of their creative imagination. Thus, before going on to contemporary literary fiction, I would like to briefly address the conflicts around sexuality in Indian mythical imagination and ancient Sanskrit poetry.

Old age in Indian cultural imagination

What are the heralds of burhapa, old age? The answer to this question is clear and consistent through centuries from ancient texts to modern ethnographic accounts which reflect Hindu life and mores. In the religious-ideal image, the curtain rises: "When a householder sees his skin wrinkled, and his hair white, and the sons of his sons, then he may resort to the forest" (Manu, n.d., p. 198).

The actual "resort to the forest"—vanaprastha—was always rare. What was being enjoined was a gradual withdrawal from family ties and family affairs, a renunciation of worldly concerns and pleasures from the previous "householder" stage of life, and an increasing involvement with spiritual, "ultimate concerns."

In the *Mahabharata*, Yuddhishtra, the eldest Pandava brother describes the psychological state of the withdrawal thus:

> Without indulging in grief or joy, and regarding censure and applause, hope and affliction, equally, and prevailing over every couple of opposites, I shall live casting off all the things of the world … Divesting myself of desire and wrath, and turning my gaze inwards, I shall go on, casting off pride of soul and body. (Vyasa, n.d., *Mahabharata*, Santiparva, Section 9: 14–18)

The crisis of renunciation versus involvement in burhapa has sexuality as a central issue. Sexual desire undermines the realization of equanimity, the cultural ego ideal of this stage of life. The sexual Torschlusspanik—panic before the closing of the gate that abruptly grips elderly men, leading to infatuation with young women and the tragic consequences of such winter–spring unions—is amply documented in the epics. In the Ramayana, king Dasharatha must banish his beloved eldest son Rama to the forest because of a rash promise he has made to Kaikeyi, his fourth and youngest wife with whom he is besotted. In the *Mahabharata*, as narrated in an earlier chapter, there is the legend of Bhishma renouncing sexual life so that his old father, the king Santanu who is infatuated with a young fisher girl, can slake his desire.

To an unsympathetic observer, Dashratha and Santanu cut faintly ridiculous figures. Sanskrit poets, on the other hand, invite a more empathic stance as they reveal the conflict raging in the older man's tortured soul. The fifth-century (?) poet Bharatrihari, who legend has it continually vacillated between renunciation and sensual indulgence, finding them equally attractive and equally flawed, is one poet who combines an old man's clarity of vision in matters of sexual passion together with his disgust in the face of such a desire that blurs clarity even as it sharpens it (Kakar, 2015):

> Her breasts—those swellings of flesh
> are compared to golden pots;
> her face—a dwelling for phlegm—
> is likened to the moon;
> her thighs—clammy with piss—
> are said to rival the elephant's trunk.
> O these poets, how they take
> this loathsome form and make it
> profound with their similitudes. (p. 213)

However old, the lure of sexuality will never let a man go; a fish flailing on the hook, Bharatrihari avers.

> Feeble, blinded, lamed, ears and tail bitten off,
> covered in wounds, pus sores flowing,
> body crawling with worms, starving, shrivelled
> neck garlanded with an alms-pot shard,
> a dog will still follow a bitch.
> Lust swats even those already dead. (p. 233)

In his stanzas to a young girl, the seventh-century poet Mayura is even more stark in depicting the dilemmas of old-age sexuality (Mayura, n.d.).

> Rearing the green flames of his tail, the
> peacock casts the hen beneath him, in the
> dust of the King's walk. He covers her,
> and we can hardly see her. She cries and he
> cries; and the copper moons in the green
> bonfire of his tail die down;
> And I am an old man.
>
> Old maker of careful stanzas as I am, I
> am also as the fishmonger's ass and smell
> to you in riot. He is insensate and
> does not care though the Royal retinue
> be passing. He climbs and is not otherwise
> contented. And he brays aloud. (pp. 109–110)

More than a millennium apart in time, vastly distant in geographical and civilizational space, contemporary Western and Indian fiction to which I now turn share with Sanskrit poets the depiction of drivenness and twinges of self-disgust that mark the sexuality of old men.

Sex and the old man

My selection of novels is arbitrary. They are more like individual case histories than a representative sample from a larger universe of the aged. My first yardstick for selection was literary merit. Although using the medium of words, literature makes one understand in unmediated immediacy—here, the nuances of sexual imagination in the elderly—in ways no exposition, including a psychoanalytic one, ever can. My second criterion was that the authors be themselves old when they created these fictional works. In other words, I wanted to make sure that the personal experience which goes into the creation of a fictional character, however transformed by imagination, should have some anchoring in the author's own emotional experiencing of old age. Or, in the language of social anthropology, that the authors be themselves participant observers in their fictional inquiry into aged sexuality. In the case of male writers, the novels that I will consider here are: *Everyman* and *The Dying Animal* by Philip Roth, *Towards the End of Time* by John Updike, *Memories of My Melancholy Whores* by Gabriel García Marquez, and *Yayati* by Vishnu Khandekar. In the case of women writers, they are *Love, Again* by Doris Lessing, *Fear of Dying* by Erica Jong, and Colette's *Cheri*.

Philip Roth's (2006a) novel *Everyman* is about a seventy-one-year-old multi-divorced, successful advertising man who is facing his physical deterioration and approaching death—without the aid of religion or philosophy. Roth wrote this book when he was himself that age. The theme of aging desire was also central to more than one of his preceding novels, such as *The Dying Animal* (2001). Indeed, in Roth's in-turn raging, impassioned, woeful voice in these novels, we keep hearing the Irish poet W. B. Yeats' (1976) mournful lines from *Sailing to Byzantium*, written at the age of sixty-one, from which the title of Roth's 2001 novel was taken, that as an aged man he was but "a paltry thing / A tattered coat upon a stick" and a soul "sick with desire / And fastened to a dying animal" (p. 191).

Roth's rage is against that arch betrayer, the body, and over the battle "to remain an unassailable man" that has been lost, "time having transformed his own body into a store-house for man-made contraptions designed to fend off collapse. Defusing thoughts of his own demise had never required more diligence and cunning" (p. 16). His productive, active way of life gone, he no longer possesses the productive man's male allure, a situation also faced by the sixty-six-year-old retired investment counselor of John Updike's *Towards the End of Time* (1997): "my professional usefulness over, my wife more of a disciplinarian than a comfort, my body a swamp in whose simmering depths a fatal infirmity must be brewing" (p. 172).

Much worse than the loss of identity as a worker, a part of masculine sex allure, the reason why the loss of a job is always more than a loss of livelihood, and the evident decay of the body, is the loss of cockiness, in its literal sense. The cock, the penis that functions erratically in the old is the focus of Roth's impotent rage in another novel, *Exit Ghost* (2006b); it is a "spigot of wrinkled flesh" (p. 103) that is

> like the end of a pipe you see sticking out of a field somewhere,
> a meaningless piece of pipe that spurts and gushes intermittently,

spitting forth water to no end, until a day arrives when somebody remembers to give the valve the extra turn that shuts the damn sluice down. (pp. 109–110)

Updike's hero distastefully regards his genitals as "lumps of obsolete purpose in wrinkled sacks of the thinnest skin" (p. 172).

The intensity of desolation at the loss of the penis' sexual functioning suggests a deeper malaise than a simple reaction to uncertain or complete loss of erections. The desolation is at the loss of a deep unconscious fantasy of the existence of the phallus, which, psychoanalysts (Benton, 1995; Birksted-Breen, 1996) would say, especially after Lacan, represents the site of (illusory) autonomy, wholeness, and total fulfillment.

While neither sex has access to the phallus, the boy's erect penis, the actual physical organ, functions as the signifier of the phallus. He can more easily believe in a privileged access to the phallus. The desolation and the impotent rage of the old men in the novels is then a consequence of being confronted with the reality of incompleteness and a giving up the fantasy of total fulfillment.

I would suggest here that the lingam, the aniconic representation of the Hindu deity Shiva, is a more appropriate and far-reaching symbol than the phallus for the representation of the psychic constellation discussed above. In its worship in countless homes, roadsides, temples, the phallus in the Shiva lingam is always represented as arising out of the yoni, the symbol of female creative energy. The lingam, then, symbolizes the unity of the male and female and the cosmic energy generated by this union. Iconically, the union is often portrayed in temple sculptures in a starkly sexual language, Shakti straddling the thighs of Shiva in a tight embrace that lasts thousands of years. In its ritual worship in temples and homes, cups of cold milk are poured on the lingam to cool the heat of the energy rising from the union. Besides symbolizing unity and vitality, myths of the lingam further elaborate on what else it symbolizes. It must be said, though, that these myths, created by men, are almost solely about the phallic aspect of the lingam, the pillar arising from the base. The female yoni at its base, often almost a part of the earth on which the lingam stands, retreats to the background in the male-created myths and is not so obviously discernible, not unlike the vagina that is tucked away between a woman's legs.

The origin myth of the lingam tells us of a quarrel between the two other gods of the Hindu trinity, Brahma and Vishnu, about who was the superior of the two when a pillar of light appeared between them. Shiva challenges them to find the two ends of the pillar. Brahma flies up and Vishnu dives down deep but no matter how far they traverse the length of the lingam, they cannot find its ends. Shiva then appears from the central part of the pillar of light; the light-filled lingam then symbolizes infinity and enlightenment when, in biblical language, man no longer sees through a glass darkly and knows not the part but the whole.

In an earlier chapter, I narrated the myth of a boy who clung tightly to the lingam when Yama, the god of death, came to take him and was unsuccessful in prying him loose. Here, the lingam represents victory over death. For the male protagonists of the novels, the sexual act, contingent upon the uncertain erections of old age, becomes much more than the straightforward matter of a "fuck." For them, nothing else, not money, not children, not achievements, can keep the conscious and unconscious fears of the approaching end as much at bay as sex. Money, family, status might help, Roth (2001) suggests, but:

> none of them are like the other thing [sex] because the other thing is based in your physical being, in the flesh that is born and the flesh that dies. Because only when you fuck is everything that you dislike in life and everything by which you are defeated in life purely, if momentarily, revenged. Only then are you most cleanly alive and most cleanly yourself. … It's not the sex that's the corruption—it's the rest. Sex isn't just friction and shallow fun. Sex is also the revenge on death. Don't forget death. Don't ever forget it. Yes, sex too is limited in its power. … But tell me, what power is greater? (p. 69)

In Vishnu Khandekar's 1960 novel, *Yayati*, written when the author was sixty-two, a retelling of the legend of King Yayati from the epic *Mahabharata*, the king's first response to aging, like many other men before and after him, is to go over moments of past pleasures with women, gathering "a rich harvest of happiness in alluring glances, tender embraces and silken heads of hair" (p. 231). The recollection of past embraces is not enough to assuage his terror of getting old and a forced renunciation of sexual pleasure. Disgusted, his father-in-law curses him to instantly lose his youth and become a decrepit old man. On his pleading, the sage relents. Yayati can have his youth back if one of his sons agrees to take on his old age, regaining his youth at his father's death. One of the sons, Puru, seeing the unhappiness of the father, offers him his own youth. Yayati is conflicted over the offer but not for long:

> All the lurking desires were drumming in my years: "There is that beautiful maiden waiting for you in your room. For the last fifteen days, you had set your heart on her. Are you going to throw away this opportunity without even putting your lips to it? What, after all, does Puru stand to lose by taking over your old age for three or four years? On the other hand, he stands to gain a kingdom. For a few years, enjoy life to your heart's content; assuage all desire and then return to him his youth." (p. 241)

At that particular moment, Yayati has no hesitation in offering his kingdom for a further extension of time to have access to the bodies of young women. In the greedy and panicked embrace of the female body, we can glimpse his terror at the loss of infinitude promised by the lingam. Updike's protagonist expresses his version of this understanding when he says that women's bodies deliver the acceptance that matters and, "Through the bodies of women men conduct what tortured dealings they can with the universe, producing serial murder and morganatic marriages and a Morgan Library's worth of love letters, novels, and death threats" (p. 59).

It is perhaps unsurprising that whether in *Everyman*, *The Dying Animal*, or *Yayati* it is the bodies of *young* women that are the source of Eros once again surging through an old body, even if for brief moments when the connection to the lingam's vitality and energy is re-established, the narrative of the novel carried forward by the consequences of this upsurge. Dirty old man, the label derisively coined by the young who find even old-age sexual imagination reprehensible, can be pinned on a large number of their fathers, grandfathers, teachers, and other venerated old men in private and public life. It is not only in Updike's retired investment counselor's dreams that "sex still revolves with surprising force, turning a phantom woman into a hairy moist center of desire, hot as a star" (p. 2).

To explore the theme of old men's sexual rejuvenation through young women further in our literary "case histories," let me begin with Roth's protagonist in *Everyman*. Every morning, he watches the

> robustly healthy young women he saw jogging along the boardwalk when he took his morning walk, still all curves and gleaming hair … Following their speedy progress with his gaze was a pleasure, but a difficult pleasure, and at bottom the mental caress was a source of biting sadness that only intensified an unbearable loneliness. (pp. 101–102)

He becomes obsessed:

> Nothing any longer kindled his curiosity or answered his needs, not his painting, not his family, not his neighbors, nothing except the young women who jogged by him on the boardwalk in the morning. My God, he thought, the man I once was! The life that surrounded me! The force that was mine! (p. 130)

One morning he stops a young woman who has particularly caught his fancy and tries to draw her into a conversation, even as:

> he tried repeatedly to prevent his gaze from falling to the swell of the breasts that rose and fell with her breathing. This was torment to walk away from. The idea was an affront to common sense and his sanity. His excitement was disproportionate to anything that had happened or that possibly could happen. … as he did his best to conceal his anxiety—and the urge to touch—and the craving for just one such body—and the futility of it all—and his insignificance—and apparently succeeded. (pp. 131–132)

The young woman does not make a face or run off laughing at him when he tells her he'd like to see her again and gives her his phone number that she accepts. He feels himself "growing hard in his pants unbelievably, magically quickly, as though he was fifteen. And feeling too, that sharp sense of individualization, of sublime singularity, that marks a fresh sexual encounter or love affair and that is the opposite of the deadening depersonalization of serious illness" (pp. 133–134). The woman never calls and doesn't jog on the same boardwalk again, thereby "thwarting his longing for the last great outburst of everything" (p. 134).

The sexual imagination of Updike's protagonist, who "seeks out only young whores, with tight lower bodies and long, exercise-hardened limbs" (p. 24), is fired by an even more insignificant encounter. A young woman at a train station accidentally turns her face toward him as she blows a bubble of bubble gum: "The primitive man within me prickled at this casual uncalled for protrusion of insolent nakedness, a roundness out of her mouth pinker and more blatant than an exposed breast or penis …" (p. 29).

Unlike the protagonists of the American novels who suffer the inevitable defeat of Eros as they fall back into the reality of old age, the poignancy of knowing that their access to the vitality and energy of lingam is forever lost, yet do not regret their moments of erotic illusion, Yayati is remorseful at the end:

> I had trampled underfoot my duty as a father. I had spurned parental sentiment and forgotten common humanity. For momentary selfish pleasure, I had sacrificed the offspring of my flesh and blood. For eighteen years, I had been raising a temple to the demon of desire. What a terrible dome I had set on it today! (p. 243)

Yet behind the voice of remorse, I can also hear another one, which is still paying obeisance to Kama, the god of desire, saying, "I will make the same choice today as I did then."

It is not that the old men of these novels are unaware of the radical inappropriateness of their desire and the disorder the stabbing of lust can bring to their inner and outer lives. In *The Dying Animal*, Professor Kepesch no longer believes in the unquestioned superiority of the rewards of the intellect. For him now, sublimation is little more than, in the poet W. H. Auden's words, "the sin of the high minded" that reason forces us to commit and which "damns the soul by praising it" (Auden, 1976, p. 248). He is fully aware of the dangerous terrain he is stepping into as he embarks on an affair with a twenty-four-year-old student, Consuela. Unlike the falling in love of youth which is almost always with the eyes shut, the eyes of older people, men and women, are wide open.

> Yet what do you do if you're sixty-two and believe you'll never have a claim on something so perfect again? … What do you do if

you're sixty-two and you realize that all those bodily parts invisible up to now (kidneys, lungs, veins, arteries, brain, intestines, prostate, heart) are about to start making themselves distressingly apparent, while the organ most conspicuous throughout your life is doomed to dwindle into insignificance? (Roth, 2001, pp. 33–34)

It is also an error to believe the old men are seeking rejuvenation by partaking the youth of their young lovers, of believing that "you are as old as the *woman* you feel." As Howard Levine (2008) emphasizes in a review of *The Dying Animal*, Kepesch is acutely aware of what an affair with Consuela will *not* do:

> Don't misunderstand me. It isn't that, through Consuela, you can delude yourself into thinking that you have a last shot at your youth. You never feel the difference from youth more. In her energy, in her enthusiasm, in her youthful unknowing, in her youthful *knowing*, the difference is dramatized every moment. … Far from feeling youthful, you feel the poignancy of her limitless future as opposed to your own limited one. (p. 34)

What Kepesch and the protagonists of the other novels do not emphasize enough is that it is not just a rejuvenation of the body and a reinvigoration of sensate responsiveness that old age passion brings them as it proceeds to connect them to the energy of the lingam. It also opens the door to a further exploration of the self as many forgotten selves begin to bubble up to the surface of the psyche. Or as the heroine of *Love, Again* (Lessing, 1997) says, "There is absolutely nothing like love for showing how many different people can live inside one skin" (p. 225). And if the love is returned, as in the case of the neurologist and writer Oliver Sacks, who fell in love with a young man at the age of seventy-five, then the consequent rediscovery of atrophied parts of the self is hugely welcome, without the torments that often accompany such discoveries (Sacks, 2015):

> There was an intense emotionality at this time: music I loved, or the long golden sunlight of late afternoon, would set me weeping. I was not sure what I was weeping for, but I would feel an intense sense of love, death, and transience, inseparably mixed. (p. 380)

As Sacks' narrative suggests, one way out of the dilemmas of men's old-age sexuality and the unbearable snapping of the link to the lingam is via the emotional rather than the physical experience of love. Likewise, Marquez's novella *Memories of My Melancholy Whores*, written when he was seventy-seven years old, suggests a relinquishing of the phallic body, although this, too, has its shortcomings.

In *Memories of My Melancholy Whores*, shortly before his ninetieth birthday, the anonymous hero of the novella, a columnist for a small-town newspaper, decides to offer himself "the gift of a night of wild love with an adolescent virgin" (p. 3).[21] The girl offered to him in the brothel is the fourteen-year-old Delgadina who works in a factory sewing buttons the whole day and is already asleep, naked, when he enters the room at night. He makes a half-hearted attempt to part her thighs but soon gives up as the girl, still asleep, turns on her side, away from him. Watching her sleeping form, "That night I discovered the improbable pleasure of contemplating the body of a sleeping woman without the urgencies of desire or the obstacles of modesty" (p. 29). When the madam of the brothel offers him a discount for his next visit since "nothing happened" on that night, he insists on repeating what had happened earlier, that the girl be asleep when he arrives, he share the bed and leave at dawn while the girl is still sleeping. An almost unbearable tenderness toward the sleeping girl, without a trace of desire is swelling up in his heart and he is "filled with a sense of liberation I hadn't known before in my life, and free at last of a servitude [to desire] that had kept me enslaved since the age of thirteen" (p. 45). He has fallen in love with the sleeping girl, a love that eschews physical consummation but has as powerful an impact on his psyche as when desire alone ruled. He feels a strong longing take hold of his soul. In my throat, "I felt the Gordian knot of all the loves that might have been and weren't" (p. 53), and "Disoriented by the merciless evocation of Delgadina asleep," the spirit of his Sunday columns changes as he now conceives of them as love letters to her, "my life poured into every word" (p. 66). He feels he is becoming another

---

[21] The story is similar to the Japanese Nobel laureate Yasunari Kawabata's (1961) novella, *House of the Sleeping Beauties*, about a grandfather who frequents a brothel where young girls are exhibited in their sleep and the grandfather is warned by the brothel keeper not to do anything in "bad taste" with a sleeping girl.

man, and goes back to the romantic writings he had repudiated when young and is convinced that the invisible power that moves the world is unrequited, not happy love.

The columnist's body is not absent in this love. But what is present is the adoring body, not the desiring one. With Delgadina still asleep:

> I kissed her all over her body until I was breathless: her spine, vertebra by vertebra, down to her languid buttocks, the side with the mole, the side of her inexhaustible heart. As I kissed her the heat of her body increased, and it exhaled a wild, untamed fragrance. She responded with new vibrations along every inch of her skin, and on each one I found a distinctive heat, a unique taste, a different moan, and her entire body resonated inside with an arpeggio, and her nipples opened and flowered without being touched. (p. 72)

Leavy (2010) is right in his observation that eroticism in the form of tender caring becomes stronger in old age but to call this a regression to infantile sexuality (Balint, 1933) may be the phallocentric bias of psychoanalysis of an early era that is rooted in Western cultural imagination.

Akin to the travails of the desiring body in old age—the humiliations, the self-disgust, the impotent rage, the deep sadness—the adoring body too suffers, in its case, the pangs of unending separation and ever-receding unity. The important difference is that for the adoring body, despair itself becomes a part of the attraction—in fact its main allure, its definition—to be embraced rather than to be recoiled from. When the girl disappears and he cannot find her, the old columnist discovers that the phrase "dying of love" is not poetic license and that he actually *felt* he was dying of love. "At the same time, the contrary was also true. I would not have traded the delights of my suffering for anything in the world" (p. 84). For fifteen years he has been trying to translate the poems of Leopardi but only now has he a profound sense of the line, "*Ah me, if this is love, then how it torments*" (p. 84).

The easier abjuring of his phallic body by the old columnist has its antecedents in his life history where the phallic narcissism, so blatant in the novels of Roth and Updike, was absent in his sexual encounters with women: "My sexual age never worried me because my powers did not depend so much on me as on women, and they know the how and the why when they want to"; the unpredictability of the erections, the varying hardness of the penis, didn't matter, "because they are the risks of being alive" (p. 10).

The adoring lover, longing for the idealized beloved, his love unrequited, is also very much a part of Japanese sexual imagination, to which the novels of the first Japanese winner of the Nobel Prize for literature Yasunari Kawabata, especially *Snow Country* (1956) and *The Sound of the Mountain* (1996), testify. In the latter novel, as in *House of the Sleeping Beauties* (it served as an inspiration for *Memories of My Melancholy Whores*, which feature old lovers), Kawabata's answer to the dilemmas of old-age sexuality owes much to a strong strain in Japanese culture that values an aesthetic contemplation of transience and sadness of things and states of mind. Zen-like, an old man must learn to do what the unrequited lover does—to drink tea from an empty cup, recollect separation in love in aesthetic tranquility.

In Marquez's novel, it appears that the old man's preferred access to the symbol of the lingam is not through the phallus but through the yoni at its base, here as the maternal genital leading to the vision of emergence and mergence that ends man's separation from a maternal universe. Like the phallic preoccupations of the central characters in Roth's and Updike's novels, the protagonist of Marquez's fiction, too, seeks only a partial access to the lingam. In his adoration of the girl who is sleeping, dead to the world, there is a denial of the yoni's sexual energy that combines with that of the phallus to make the lingam a symbol of cosmic creative energy.

Sexuality and the older woman

Sexuality in the older woman is at higher risk of social censure than in a man, hidden not only from the world but generally also from herself. As the narrator of Doris Lessing's novel *Love, Again* (written when the author was seventy-eight), observes:

> Most men and more women—young women afraid for themselves— punish older women with derision, punish them with cruelty, when they show inappropriate signs of sexuality. If men, they are getting their own back for the years they have been subject to the sexual power of women. (1997, p. 133)

My clinical impression is that the tendency to punish aged female sexuality is even stronger among many Indian men because of the continued presence in their psyche of what I have called "maternal enthrallment" (Kakar, 2016), especially its third constituent: incestuous desire coexisting with the terror inspired by an overwhelming female sexuality.

The older woman may claim in good faith that she is satisfied with getting older, pleased that the emotional tumults of sexual love are behind her, yet she is not immune to the stabbings of desire. Kama, the Hindu god of love, can bring her to grief by aiming arrows at a young heart within an old body, at an unchanged core fenced in by wilting flesh.

Sarah Durham, the heroine of *Love, Again*, an educated widow of sixty-five who is the successful manager of a theatre, believes she is in a serene stage of her life where she is able to concentrate undistracted upon fulfilling work. Yet her whole psychic equilibrium goes for a toss when she falls in love with a young actor who is superficial and has little to recommend him except a surfeit of charm which, she is aware, always promises more than it can deliver. Sarah both revels and hurts in the sensate openness that the falling in love has brought in its wake. Music, the language of emotions, has a special power over her mood so that even a banal and silly tune can make her cry. Words or phrases connected with love, passion that she would have earlier found stupid, can bring her to tears. Daydreams begin to take over her waking life, to be pushed away with effort before, succumbing, she spends hours daydreaming as in the first flush of youth.

Once the older woman discovers, often against her conscious intent, that the door to Eros is again open and, in fact, was never shut, she falls into the same agonizing self-interrogation as the older man but with one significant difference: the focus of her anguish is not her genitals but the whole body. And it is through the mirror, standing in for the eyes of an actual or fantasized lover, that the woman conducts this conversation with herself on her sexual allure, a conversation from which the vagina, hidden in her body as it is from the lover's eyes, is absent, of little cause for concern or distress in her sexual imagination:

> A woman of a certain age stands in front of her looking-glass naked, examining this or that part of her body. She has not done this for … twenty years? Thirty? Her left shoulder, which

she pushes forward, to see it better—not bad at all. She always did have good shoulders. And a very good back ... Hard to see her back, though: it was not a big mirror. Her breasts? A good many young women would be pleased to have them. But wait ... what had happened to them? ... the last thing anyone thought of, looking at them, was nourishment, but they have become comfortable paps ... Legs. Well, they weren't too bad now, never mind what they were. In fact her body had been a pretty good one, and it held its shape (more or less) till she moved, when a subtle disintegration set in, and areas shapely enough were surfaced with the fine velvety wrinkles of an elderly peach. But all this was irrelevant. What she could not face was that any girl at all, no matter how ill-favoured, had one thing she had not. And would never have again. It was the irrevocableness of it, there was nothing to be done. She had lived her way into this, and to say, "Well, and so does everyone," did not help. (pp. 242–243)

The poignancy of her self-regard is deepened by the fact that the body she is looking at is not the one she has now but is accompanied by another.

She glanced at her forearm, bare because of the heat, shapely still but drying out, seeing it simultaneously as it was now and as it had been then. This body of hers, in which she was living comfortably enough, was accompanied by another, her young body, shaped in a kind of ectoplasm. (p. 97)

The mirror is also the confidante (and the enemy) of Lea, a former courtesan and heroine of Colette's (1920) novel *Cheri*, who is having an affair with a twenty-five-year-old man half her age. Looking closely into the mirror, she observes her hair, which is badly dyed red and has roots that are turning white. She wonders about draping it prudently or otherwise completely hiding the withered neck that is encircled by large wrinkles. She even thinks of changing her hairdo, which she has worn high for twenty years and which showed the back of her neck. Sunlight "fell also on the soft flabby skin on the back of her well-shaped hands and her wrists. This emphasized—like criss-crossings on a clay soil when heavy rain is followed by a dry spell—the complicated network of tiny concentric grooves and miniature parallelograms" (p. 114). At another time, "Not yet powdered, a meager twist of hair at the back of her head, double chin, and raddled neck, she was exposing herself rashly to the unseen observer" (p. 111). Her only, rueful consolation is that she notices, "as the skin gets less firm, the scent sinks in better and lasts much longer" (pp. 94–95).

What the older woman mourns in the loss of a youthful body is not only a narcissistic impoverishment that is also the lot of older men, but almost as important, her loss of sexual power over male desire. Erica Jong's (2015) heroine in *Fear of Dying*, written when the author was seventy-three years old, vividly testifies to the acuity of this loss:

> I used to love the power I had over men. Walking down the street, my mandolin-shaped ass swaying and swinging to their backward eyes. How strange that I only completely knew this power when it was gone—or transferred to my daughter, all male eyes on her nubile twentyish body … I missed this power. It seemed that the things that had come to replace it—marriage, maternity, the wisdom of the mature woman … weren't worth the candle. (p. 5)

Lessing, too, muses on this power, which she traces back to the first steps a girl takes into womanhood, its importance for women's sexuality and erotic imagination, and what the loss of this power entails for the older woman:

> she remembered walking across a room knowing that everyone watched her, holding herself as if filled to the brim with a precious and dangerous fluid. Young girls do this, when they first discover their power: luckily most do not know how much they have. What can be more entertaining than to watch some grub of a girl, thirteen years old or so, astonished when a man (old as far as she is concerned) starts to stammer and go red, showing the nervous aggression that goes with unwelcome attraction. What's all this? she thinks, and then is seized with illumination. Her wings burst forth, and she walks smiling across a room, reckless with power. And this condition can last until middle age deflates her. (1997, p. 96)

The deflation is worse, the loss of sexual power more acute, in case of the woman whose youth was augmented by that mysterious entity called "sex appeal." No longer a member of the privileged class sexually, which she had been once, she now finds herself being one of "millions who spend their lives behind ugly masks, longing for the simplicities of love known to attractive people" (p. 141).

Her desert of deprivation seems more formidable and unforgiving than the one in which millions of unattractive people live out most of their lives, becoming familiar with and contenting themselves to eke out an existence on the meager sustenance the sexual desert offers them.

If sexual power, intimately connected to her physical allure, is central to woman's sexual imagination and response, then it is comprehensible that the hardness of the cock, the erection of the penis, does not play as important a role in the woman's sexuality as men would like to believe. I do not mean to imply that it plays no role; not at all. Erica Jong's heroine puts it succinctly:

> Erection—how we all seek it! The hard cock standing up and validating our existence. Men think like this—straight men and gay men both. And women do too—at least when hunger drives us. But does this hardness have anything to do with our charm and sex appeal? (2015, p. 6)

The hardness of the cock, then, not as an ode by the man to his own desire but as his homage to the woman's allure, not a promiscuous erection but a testimony to her sexual power over him, can further fuel a woman's own desire. This is critical for the sexuality of the older woman once her initial sexual hunger has abated. Aware of the loss of her sexual allure, images of her own charms can no longer fuel her sexual passion as "they once had when she had been almost as much intoxicated with herself as with the male body that loved hers" (Lessing, 1997, p. 143). Under the complaint of absence of the hard cock, both Jong and Lessing are bemoaning the incompleteness at the loss of the lingam, of being deprived of the fantasized possibility of bisexual wholeness.[22]

Desire and longing in old age: Cultural aspects

In Saul Bellow's last novel (2000), the philosopher Ravelstein, close to death, proclaims love to be "our species' highest vocation" (p. 120). In its neediness and awareness of incompleteness, in its longing for

---

[22] For the bisexual wholeness symbolized by the lingam see Kakar, 1978, p. 158.

bisexual wholeness and its promise of ecstasy, vitality, and liveliness beyond the ordinary, love combines the elemental forces of desire and longing, akin to Freud's sensuality and tenderness—*Sinnlichkeit* and *Zaertlichkeit* (Freud, 1912d, p. 180). At another place (Kakar & Ross, 1986), I have described desire as the stream in which the body's wanting and its violence, the mind's yearning for sexual pleasure but also the need to rid itself of ancient pain and noxious hate, the excitement of the orgasm and the fierce exultation of possession, all flow together (p. 199). In longing, on the other hand, what the lover aspires to is submission, surrender to the beloved, not possession. He would be a slave, not the master; he would rather adore the beloved's body than fold it into a passionate embrace. What the lover yearns for is for his soul to merge with that of the beloved in an ineffable union that is impossible as long as he has a body. Identifying his longing with the totality of love, for him "sex is the consolation you have when you can't have love" (Marquez, 2006, p. 69).

Love, of course, is neither longing nor desire alone but a river in which both streams flow together. Hence, the power and glory of the sexual embrace with a beloved person that delivers the "double whammy": the desire of the body combined with the longing of the soul.

Men, not only aged ones, range themselves on different points of the continuum of longing and desire. At one end, where desire alone rules, phallic narcissism is at its height, and less than conscious rage and despair boil under the surface of an enforced renunciation of old age. At the other end, where longing alone holds sway, men seek to jettison the phallic body and embrace femininity, their partner's and their own, so as to become one with the feminine body of the beloved. The torment here is the realization of an elemental separation that can never be undone, of the lover being compelled (to adapt the poet W. H. Auden's phrase) to count up to two when he longs to be able to count up to one (Auden, 1973, p. 24).

Older women, too, occupy different positions on the continuum. At one end, where desire alone rules, there is a resignation and disappointment in the unavailability of the phallus. At the other end where longing reigns there is a vain quest for the end of exile.

From the experience of unsatisfied longing, Lessing's Sarah Durham reflects on whether longing comes from childhood injury or whether it has a deeper locus. In one of her reflections, she singles out earliest life as that which gives drive to longing:

> That baby is wanting more: it is longing for something just out of its memory; it is longing for where it came from, and when need starts up in its stomach for milk, that need revives another, grander need, just as a small girl may pause in her play, look up, see a sky aflame with sunset and sadness, and find herself stretching up her arms to that lost magnificence and sobbing because she is so utterly exiled. (1997, p. 350)

Lessing's reflection returns us to that central psychoanalytic preoccupation: early childhood, the part of life that had so interested Freud, in which desire and instinctual life are present but not goal-directed (Freud, 1905a, p. 150). It opens up the question of whether some kind of primal longing is the fount of erotic desire, a desire that differentiates out of longing in infancy and for which the mother, and eventually the parents, become the first repositories, but that has a life and purpose of its own that parallels the life stages, beginning with autoeroticism, moving into genital eroticism, and closing, if one is lucky, with an investment in an eroticism of spiritual life.

Like individuals, cultures, too, occupy different points on the longing–desire continuum based on the meaning and value that they place on the experience of exile and the possibilities they invest in the act of longing. Cultures that embrace the body and materiality as the ultimate truth, and death as the final end, may be more likely to take positions resembling the little boy who holds on to the phallus. These range from a valorizing of the phallic body of desire (Roth's and Updike's novels) or to the resigned acceptance of death as a cure for the loss of love in old people, as Lessing's character puts it: "When Cupid aims arrows (not flowers or kisses) at the elderly and old, and brings them to grief, is this one way of hustling people who are in danger of living too long off the stage?" (p. 350).

Cultures that value the spiritual as much as the material might be more likely to valorize longing that goes beyond the body. These are cultures that hold up a prototype of the ideal lover who is almost identical with the hero of Marquez's novella. In some of these cultures, such as the Persian-Islamic one with which I am somewhat familiar,

Majnun, the hero of the twelfth-century Persian poet Nizami's tale of Layla and Majnun, continues to exercise an undimmed fascination (Kakar & Ross, 1986). Driven to the point of madness in an enforced separation from his beloved, he refuses to physically consummate his love even when the opportunity arises. Only by renunciation of his phallic body can he seek the psychic–spiritual unity with his beloved Layla, even as he embraces the torments of separation from her as a sign that he is on the right path in his quest toward allaying a primal longing. Similarly, in most cultures of the Indian subcontinent, longing continues to exercise a psychic pull which is explicit in Sanskrit poetry (as also in Tamil poetry) of ancient India where the love-in-separation, *viraha*, is seen as superior to love-in-union, *shringara*; the sadness of longing is a loftier sentiment than the gratification of desire.

References

Abraham, K. (1909). *Dreams and Myths: A Study in Race Psychology*. New York: Journal of Nervous and Mental Health Publishing Company, 1913.

Adams, V. (1976, August 14). Freud's work thrives as theory, not therapy. *The New York Times*.

Agarwal, M. (2000). *Sai Ek, Roop Anek* ("Sai is one but forms are many"). Calcutta, India: Sri Satya Sai Book and Publications Trust.

Ainslie, R. C. (2018). Boundaries and representation in the Mexico-Texas borderland: Reflections on geography, culture, and identity. *Journal of the American Psychoanalytic Association, 66*: 767–776.

Akhtar, S. (2005). *Freud Along the Ganges*. New York: Other Press.

Akhtar, S. (2008). *The Crescent and the Couch*. Lanham, MD: Jason Aronson.

Akhtar, S. (2009). *Freud and the Far East*. Lanham, MD: Jason Aronson.

Alexander, F. (1931). Buddhist training as an artificial catatonia. *Psychoanalytic Review, 18*: 129–145.

Altman, N. (1995). *The Analyst in the Inner City: Race, Class, and Culture Through a Psychoanalytic Lens*. Hillsdale, NJ: The Analytic Press.

Altman, N. (2000). Black and white thinking: A psychoanalyst reconsiders race. *Psychoanalytic Dialogues, 10*: 589–605.

Anandalakshmi, S. (Ed.) (1994). *The Girl Child and Her Family*. New Delhi: Dept. of Women and Child Development, HRD Ministry.

Anderson, W., Jenson, D., & Keller, R. C. (2012). *Unconscious Dominions: Psychoanalysis, Colonial Trauma, and Global Sovereignties*. Durham, NC: Duke University Press.

Auden, W. H. (1973). *Forewords and Afterwords*. London: Faber and Faber.

Auden, W. H. (1976). In sickness and health. In: *Collected Poems* (pp. 247–249). New York: Random House.

Balint, M. (1933). The psychological problems of growing old. In: *Problems of Human Pleasure and Behavior*. New York: Liveright, 1957.

Balint, M. (1979). *The Basic Fault: Therapeutic Aspects of Regression*. London: Tavistock.

Basch-Kahre, E. (1984). On difficulties arising in transference and counter-transference when analyst and analysand have different socio-cultural backgrounds. *International Review of Psycho-Analysis, 11*: 61–67.

Bateson, G. (1972). *Steps to an Ecology of Mind*. Chicago, IL: University of Chicago Press, 2000.

Bellamy, A. (2019). Trauma, fragmentation and narrative: Sandor Ferenczi's relevance for psychoanalytical perspectives on our response to climate change and environmental destruction. *International Journal of Applied Psychoanalytic Studies, 16*: 100–108.

Bellow, S. (2000). *Ravelstein*. New York: Viking Penguin.

Benton, R. J. (1995). The Aufhebung of the phallus. *Psychoanalysis & Contemporary Thought, 18*(1): 53–74.

Bergeret, J. (1993). Psychanalyse et universalité interculturelle. *Revue Française de Psychanalyse, 57*(3): 809–840.

Berkeley-Hill, O. (1921). The anal-erotic factor in the religion, philosophy and character of the Hindus. *International Journal of Psychoanalysis, 2*: 306–338.

Bion, W. R. (1967). Notes on memory and desire. *Psychoanalytic Forum, 2*: 271–280.

Birksted-Breen, D. (1996). Phallus, penis and mental space. *International Journal of Psychoanalysis, 77*: 649–657.

Bollas, C. (1979). The transformational object. *International Journal of Psychoanalysis, 60*: 97–107.

Bollas, C. (1992). *Being a Character: Psychoanalysis and Self Experience*. New York: Hill & Wang.

Bolognini, S. (2001). Empathy and the unconscious. *Psychoanalytic Quarterly, LXX*: 447–471.

Bose, G. (1948). A new theory of mental life. *Samiksa, 2*: 108–205.

Bose, G. (1949). The genesis and adjustment of the Oedipus wish. *Samiksa, 3*: 222–240.

Bose, G. (1950). The genesis of homosexuality. *Samiksa, 4*: 66–85.

Brickman, H. R. (1998). The psychoanalytic cure and its discontents: A Zen Buddhist perspective on "common unhappiness" and the polarized self. *Psychoanalysis & Contemporary Thought, 21*: 3–32.

Buie, D. (1981). Empathy: Its nature and limitations. *Journal of the American Psychoanalytic Association, 30*: 959–978.

Cath, S., & Miller, N. E. (1986). The psychoanalysis of the older patient. *Journal of the American Psychoanalytic Association, 34*: 163–177.

Chittick, W. C. (1983). *The Sufi Path of Love: The Spiritual Teachings of Rumi.* Albany, NY: SUNY Press.

Clement, C. (2005). The evocation of death anxiety on a meditation retreat. *Psychoanalytic Dialogues, 15*: 139–152.

Cohen, G. (2005). *The Mature Mind: The Positive Power of the Aging Brain.* New York: Basic Books.

Colette (1920). *Cheri.* R. Stenhouse (Trans.). London: Vintage, 2001.

Coltart, N. E. (1991). The analysis of an elderly patient. *International Journal of Psychoanalysis, 72*: 209–219.

Courtright, P. (1986). *Ganesa.* New York: Oxford University Press.

Dalal, F. (2002). *Race, Color, and the Processes of Racialization.* London: Brunner-Routledge.

Dalal, F. (2006) Racism: Processes of detachment, dehumanization, and hatred. *Psychoanalytic Quarterly, 75*: 131–161.

Danil, L. R. (2020). On facing the crucial psychosocial and political-economic dimensions of anthropogenic global warming. *Psychoanalysis, Culture & Society, 25*: 271–282.

Davidson, L. (1988). Culture and psychoanalysis. *Contemporary Psychoanalysis, 24*(1): 74–91.

Deutsch, H. (1926). Okkulte Vorgaenge waehrend der Psychoanalyse. *Imago, 12*: 418–433.

Deutsch, H. (1989). On satisfaction, happiness and ecstasy. *International Journal of Psychoanalysis, 70*: 715–723.

Devereux, G. (1953). Cultural factors in psychoanalytic therapy. *Journal of the American Psychoanalytic Association, 1*: 629–655.

Devereux, G. (1978). *Ethnopsychoanalysis,* Berkeley, CA: University of California Press.

Devès, M. H. (2018). The ecological war: A reflection on the conflictive dimension of humankind's relations with its environment. *International Journal of Psychoanalysis, 99*: 1391–1408.

Dhar, A. K. (2018). Girindrasekhar Bose and the history of psychoanalysis in India. *Indian Journal of History of Science, 53*(4): 198–204.

Dickinson, E. (1861). The loneliness one dare not sound. In: T. Johnson (Ed.), *The Complete Poems of Emily Dickinson.* Boston, MA: Little Brown, 1960.

Doi, T., & Schwaber, E. A. (2016). Chapter 1: Psychoanalysis and the Japanese personality; Chapter 2: Psychoanalysis and Western man; Chapter 3: Amae and transference-love; Chapter 4: Heeding the vocabulary of another culture: Psychoanalysis in Japan. *Psychoanalytic Inquiry, 36*: 171–186.

Doolittle, H. (1956). *Tribute to Freud.* New York: Pantheon.

Egnor, M. (1986). The ideology of love in a Tamil family. In: *Divine Passions* (pp. 38–64). Berkeley, CA: University of California Press.

Ehrenzweig, A. (1964). The undifferentiated matrix of artistic identification. In: W. Muensterberger & S. Axelrad (Eds.), *The Psychoanalytic Study of Society, Vol. 3*. New York: International Universities Press.

Eigen, M. (1981). The area of faith in Winnicott, Lacan and Bion. *International Journal of Psychoanalysis, 62*: 413–433.

Eigen, M. (2001). Mysticism and psychoanalysis. *Psychoanalytic Review, 88*: 455–481.

Epstein, M. (1990). Beyond the oceanic feeling. *International Review of Psycho-Analysis, 17*: 159–164.

Erikson, E. H. (1950). *Childhood and Society*. New York: W. W. Norton.

Erikson, E. H. (1987). Personal communication.

Eyre, D. P. (1978). Identification and empathy. *International Review of Psycho-Analysis, 5*: 351–359.

Fancher, R. T. (1993). Psychoanalysis as culture. *Issues in Psychoanalytic Psychology, 15*(2): 81–93.

Ferenczi, S. (1933). Confusion of tongues between adults and the child—the language of tenderness and of passion. *Contemporary Psychoanalysis, 24*: 196–206 (1988).

Fingarette, H. (1958). Ego and mythic selflessness. *Psychoanalytic Review, 45*: 5–40.

Freud, S. (1905a). On psychotherapy. *S. E., 7*. London: Hogarth.

Freud, S. (1908e). Creative writers and day-dreaming. *S. E., 9*. London: Hogarth.

Freud, S. (1912d). On the universal tendency to debasement in the sphere of love. *S. E., 11*. London: Hogarth.

Freud, S. (1912–13). *Totem and Taboo. S. E., 13*. London: Hogarth.

Freud, S. (1916a). On transience. *S. E., 14*. London: Hogarth.

Freud, S. (1919h). The "uncanny". *S. E., 17*. London: Hogarth.

Freud, S. (1921c). *Group Psychology and the Analysis of the Ego. S. E., 18*. London: Hogarth.

Freud, S. (1923a). Two encyclopaedia articles. *S. E., 18*. London: Hogarth.

Freud, S. (1927c). *The Future of an Illusion. S. E., 21*. London: Hogarth.

Freud, S. (1930a). Civilization and Its Discontents. *S. E., 21*. London: Hogarth.

Freud, S. (1933a). New Introductory Lectures on Psycho-analysis. *S. E., 22*. London: Hogarth.

Freud, S. (1941d). Psychoanalysis and telepathy. *S. E., 18*. London: Hogarth.

Friedman, S. S. (1981). *Psyche Reborn: The Emergence of H.D.* Bloomington, IN: Indiana University Press.

Fromm, E. (1960). Psychoanalysis and Zen Buddhism. In: D. T. Suzuki, E. Fromm, & R. De Martino (Eds.), *Zen Buddhism and Psycho-analysis* (pp. 77–141). New York: Harper.

Frosch, S. (2013). *Hauntings: Psychoanalysis and Ghostly Transmissions*. London: Palgrave.

Gandhi, M. K. (1958). *The Selected Works of Mahatma Gandhi (Vol. V)*. Ahmedabad, India: Navjivan.

Gardner, F. (1999). The colonial inheritance in theory and practice. *Psychoanalytic Psychotherapy, 13*: 135–149.

Ghent, E. (1990). Masochism, submission, surrender—masochism as a perversion of surrender. *Contemporary Psychoanalysis, 26*: 108–136.

Greenson, R. (1960). Empathy and its vicissitudes. *International Journal of Psychoanalysis, 41*: 418–424.

Grotstein, J. S. (1981). Wilfred R. Bion: The man, the psychoanalyst, the mystic. A perspective on his life and work. *Contemporary Psychoanalysis, 17*: 501–536.

Grubrich-Simitis, I. (1986). Six letters of Sigmund Freud and Sandor Ferenczi on the interrelationship of psycho-analytic theory and technique. *International Review of Psycho-Analysis, 13*: 259–277.

Haidt, J. (2012). *The Righteous Mind: Why Good People Are Divided by Politics and Religion*. New York: Pantheon.

Hallstrom, L. L. (1999). *Mother of Bliss: Anandamayi Ma*. New Delhi: Oxford University Press.

Hartnack, C. (2001). *Psychoanalysis in Colonial India*. New Delhi: Oxford University Press.

Heinrich, J., Heine, S. J., & Norenzayan, A. (2010). Most people are not WEIRD. *Nature, 466*(29).

Hiltenbeitel, A. (2018). *Freud's India*. New York: Oxford University Press.

Hinze, E. (1987). Transference and countertransference in the psychoanalytic treatment of older patients. *International Review of Psycho-Analysis, 14*: 465–474.

Horton, P. C. (1974). The mystical experience: Substance of an illusion. *Journal of the American Psychoanalytic Association, 22*: 364–380.

Jackson, S. (1968). Panel on aspects of culture in psychoanalytic theory and practice. *Journal of the American Psychoanalytic Association, 16*: 651–670.

Jacobs, T. J. (1973). Posture, gesture and movement in the analyst: Cues to interpretation and countertransference. *Journal of the American Psychoanalytic Association, 21*: 72–92.

Jacobs, T. J. (1994). Non-verbal communications: Some reflections on their role in the psychoanalytic process and psychoanalytic education. *Journal of the American Psychoanalytic Association, 42*: 741–762.

Jacobs, T. J. (1995). When the body speaks: Psychoanalytic meaning in kinetic clues. *Psychoanalytic Quarterly, 64*: 784–788.

James, W. (1902). *The Varieties of Religious Experience*. New York: Longmans, Green.

Jayakar, P. (1986). *J. Krishnamurti: A Biography*. New Delhi: Penguin.

Jong, E. (2015). *Fear of Dying*. New York: St. Martin's.

Junkers, G. (2006). Is it too late? Key papers on psychoanalysis and ageing. *International Journal of Psychoanalysis Key Papers Series*. London: Karnac.

Kakar, S. (1978). *The Inner World: Childhood and Society in India*. New Delhi: Oxford University Press.

Kakar, S. (1982). *Shamans, Mystics and Doctors*. New York: Alfred A. Knopf.

Kakar, S. (1987b). Psychoanalysis and non-western cultures. *International Review of Psycho-Analysis*, *12*: 441–448.

Kakar, S. (1989). The maternal-feminine in Indian psychoanalysis. *International Review of Psycho-Analysis*, *16*(3): 355–362.

Kakar, S. (1991). *The Analyst and the Mystic*. Chicago, IL: University of Chicago Press.

Kakar, S. (1995). Clinical work and cultural imagination. *Psychoanalytic Quarterly*, *64*: 265–281.

Kakar, S. (1997). *Culture and Psyche*. New Delhi: Oxford University Press.

Kakar, S. (2015). *The Devil Take Love*. New Delhi: Hamish Hamilton.

Kakar, S. (2016). The engulfing mother in Indian mythology: Masculinity and conflicting desires. *Antyajaa: Indian Journal of Women and Social Change*, *1*: 60–64.

Kakar, S. (2018). Emotional transformation: Learnings from psychoanalysis and Buddhism. In: G. Lhakdor & B. Johnson (Eds.), *Transforming and Regulating Emotions*. Dharamshala, India: Library of Tibetan Works.

Kakar, S., & Narayanan, A. (2023). The capacious Freud. In: F. Busch & N. Delgado (Eds.), *On Freud's "The Ego and the Id"*. London:Routledge.

Kakar, S., & Ross., J. M. (1986). *Tales of Love, Sex and Danger*. New York: Blackwell.

Kassouf, S. (2017). Psychoanalysis and climate change: Revisiting Searles's The Nonhuman Environment, rediscovering Freud's Phylogenetic Fantasy, and imagining a future. *American Imago*, *74*: 141–171.

Kawabata, Y. (1956). *Snow Country*. E. G. Seidensticker (Trans.). New York: Alfred A. Knopf.

Kawabata, Y. (1961). *House of the Sleeping Beauties and Other Stories*. E. G. Seidensticker (Trans.). Palo Alto, CA: Kodansha, 2004.

Kawabata, Y. (1996). *The Sound of the Mountain*. E. G. Seidensticker (Trans.). New York: Vintage.

Keats, J. (1958). *Letters of John Keats*. H. E. Rollins (Ed.). Cambridge, MA: Harvard University Press.

Khandekar, V. S. (1960). *Yayati: A Classical Tale of Lust*. New Delhi: Orient Paperbacks, 2016.

Khanna, R. (2003). *Dark Continents: Psychoanalysis and Colonialism*. Durham, NC: Duke University Press.

Kierkegaard, S. (1844). *The Concept of Dread*. Princeton, NJ: Princeton University Press.

King, P. H. M. (1980). The life cycle as indicated by the nature of the transference in the psychoanalysis of the middle-aged and elderly. *International Journal of Psychoanalysis, 61*: 153–160.

Knight, J. A. (1987). The spiritual as a creative force in the person. *Journal of the American Academy of Psychoanalysis, 15*: 365–382.

Kohut, H. (1959). Introspection, empathy, and psychoanalysis—an examination of the relationship between mode of observation and theory. *Journal of the American Psychoanalytic Association, 7*: 459–483.

Kohut, H. (1971). *The Analysis of the Self*. New York: International Universities Press.

Kohut, H. (1977). *The Restoration of the Self*. Chicago, IL: University of Chicago Press.

Kohut, H. (1979). The two analyses of Mr Z. *International Journal of Psychoanalysis, 60*: 3–27.

Kohut, H. (1984). *How Analysis Cures*. Chicago, IL: University of Chicago Press.

Kubie, L. S. (1937). The fantasy of dirt. *Psychoanalytic Quarterly, 6*: 388–425.

Kumar, M., Dhar, A., & Mishra, A. (2018). *Psychoanalysis from the Indian Terroir: Emerging Themes in Culture, Family, and Childhood*. Lanham, MD: Rowman & Littlefield.

Lannoy, R. (1971). *The Speaking Tree*. London: Oxford University Press.

Layton, L. (2006). Racial identities, racial enactments, and normative unconscious processes. *Psychoanalytic Quarterly, 75*: 237–269.

Leavy, S. A. (1970). John Keats' psychology of creative imagination. *Psychoanalytic Quarterly, 39*: 173–197.

Leavy, S. A. (2010). *Growing Old: A Journey of Self-Discovery*. D. Alcorn (Trans.). New York: Routledge.

Lertzman, R. (2010). Psychoanalysis, culture, society and our biotic relations: Introducing an ongoing theme on environment and sustainability. *Psychoanalysis, Culture & Society, 15*: 113–116.

Lombardozzi, A. (2021). Climate change and environmental crisis: Psychoanalytic thoughts towards an anthropological ecology. *Italian Psychoanalytic Annual, 15*: 57–71.

Lessing, D. (1997). *Love, Again*. New York: Harper Collins.

Levine, H. B. (2008). Mortal combat: The tragic vision of Philip Roth. *Journal of the American Psychoanalytic Association, 56*(1): 283–293.

Levy, S. (1985). Empathy and psychoanalytic technique. *Journal of the American Psychoanalytic Association, 33*: 353–378.

Levy, I. (2011). The Laius complex: From myth to psychoanalysis. *International Forum of Psychoanalysis, 20*: 222–228.

Mahabharata (3rd C. BC–4th C. CE). J. A. B. van Buitenen (Trans.). Chicago, IL: University of Chicago Press, 1973.

Mahony, P. (2012, April 10). Personal communication.

Manu (n.d.). Manusmriti. *Sacred Books of the East: The Laws of Manus.* Vol. XXV. G. Bühler (Trans.). Oxford: Clarendon, 1886.

Margulies, A. (1993). The empathic imagination: Empathy and inscapes. *Journal of the American Academy of Psychoanalysis, 21*: 513–524.

Margulies, A. (2014). Imagining the real: An essay on Sudhir Kakar's "Culture and Psyche: A Personal Journey". In: M. Kumar, A. Dhar, & A. Mishra (Eds.), *Psychoanalysis from the Indian Terroir: Emerging Themes in Culture, Family and Childhood.* Lanham, MD: Lexington.

Maroda, K. (1999). *Seduction, Surrender, and Transformation: Emotional Engagement in the Analytic Process.* Hillsdale, NJ: The Analytic Press.

Marquez, G. G. (2006). *Memories of My Melancholy Whores.* New York: Vintage.

Marriott, M. (1976). Hindu transactions: Diversity without duality. In: B. Kapferer (Ed.), *Transactions and Meaning* (pp. 109–142). Philadelphia, PA: Institute for the Study of Human Issues.

Masson, J. M. (1980). *The Oceanic Feeling: The Origins of Religious Sentiment in Ancient India.* Dordrecht, the Netherlands: Reidel.

Mayura (n.d.). Amores of Mayura. In: E. Power-Mathys (Ed.), *Eastern Love, vol ii.* London: John Rodker, 1929.

Meissner, W. W. (1984). *Psychoanalysis and Religious Experience.* New Haven, CT: Yale University Press.

Mishan, J. (1996). Psychoanalysis and environmentalism: First thoughts. *Psychoanalytic Psychotherapy, 10*: 59–70.

Mitchell, S. A., & Harris, A. (2004). What's American about American psycho-analysis? *Psychoanalytic Dialogues, 14*: 165–191.

Moeller, M. L. (1977). Self and object in countertransference. *International Journal of Psychoanalysis, 58*: 356–376.

Moses, I. (1988). The misuse of empathy in psychoanalysis. *Contemporary Psychoanalysis, 24*: 577–594.

Muktananda, S. (1983). *The Perfect Relationship.* Ganeshpuri, India: Guru Siddha Vidyapeeth.

Nandy, A. (1995). *The Savage Freud and Other Essays.* Princeton, NJ: Princeton University Press.

Narayanan, A. (2013). Ambivalent subjects: Psychoanalysis, women's sexuality in India and the writings of Sudhir Kakar. *Psychodynamic Practice, 20*(3): 213–227.

Narayanan, A. (2018). When the enthralled mother dreams: A clinical and cultural composition. In: M. Kumar, A. Dhar, & A. Mishra (Eds.), *Psychoanalysis from the Indian Terroir: Emerging Themes in Culture, Family and Childhood.* Lanham, MD: Lexington.

Narayanan, A. (2023). *In A Rapture of Distress: Women's Sexuality and Modern India.* New Delhi: Oxford University Press.

Newberg, A. (2018). *Neurotheology*. New York: Columbia University Press.

Nisbett, R. E., & Miyamoto, Y. (2005). The influence of culture: Holistic versus analytic perception. *Trends in Cognitive Sciences, 9*(10): 467–473.

Nossiter, J. (2009). *Liquid Memory: Why Wine Matters*. New York: Farrar, Straus & Giroux.

Nurbakhsh, D. (1978). Sufism and psychoanalysis. *International Journal of Social Psychiatry, 24*(3): 204–219.

Oberoi, H. (2019). Singing to the tune of feminine desire: Crucial strands from the melody of mother–daughter relationship. Presentation at the Second COWAP Conference (International Psychoanalytic Conference), Kolkata, November 22 and 23.

Obeyesekere, G. (1981). *Medusa's Hair*. Chicago, IL: University of Chicago Press.

Obeyesekere, G. (1984). *The Cult of the Goddess Pattini*. Chicago, IL: University of Chicago Press.

Ogden, T. (1997). Reverie and metaphor. *International Journal of Psychoanalysis, 78*: 719–732.

Okinogi, K. (2009). Psychoanalysis in Japan. In: S. Akhtar (Ed.), *Freud and the Far East* (pp. 9–26). Lanham, MD: Jason Aronson.

Pigman, G. (1995). Freud and the history of empathy. *International Journal of Psychoanalysis, 76*: 237–256.

Plotkin, D. A. (2014). Older adults and psychoanalytic treatment: It's about time. *Psychodynamic Psychiatry, 42*(1): 23–50.

Pollock, G. H. (1982). On ageing and psychopathology—discussion of Dr. Norman A. Cohen's paper "On loneliness and the ageing process". *International Journal of Psychoanalysis, 63*: 275–281.

Ramanujan, A. K. (1999). *The Collected Essays of A. K. Ramanujan*. V. Dharwadekar (Ed.). New Delhi: Oxford University Press.

Randall, R. (2009). Loss and climate change: The cost of parallel narratives. *Ecopsychology, 3*: 118–129.

Reich, A. (1966). Empathy and countertransference. In: *Psychoanalytic Contributions* (pp. 344–360). New York: International Universities Press, 1973.

Rendon, M. (1993). The psychoanalysis of ethnicity and the ethnicity of psychoanalysis. *American Journal of Psychoanalysis, 53*(2): 109–122.

Róheim, G. (1950). *Psychoanalysis and Anthropology: Culture, Personality and the Unconscious*. New York: International Universities Press.

Roland, A. (1980). Psychoanalytic perspectives on personality development in India. *International Journal of Psychoanalysis, 7*: 73–87.

Ross, J. M. (1982). Oedipus Revisited—Laius and the "Laius Complex". *Psychoanalytic Study of the Child 37*: 169-200.

Ross, J. M. (1994). *What Men Want*. Cambridge, MA: Harvard University Press.

Ross, J. M. (1995). Commentary on "The impact of boundary violations in colleagues and family members". *Journal of the American Psychoanalytic Association, 43*(4): 959–961.

Ross, N. (1975). Affect as cognition: with observations on the meaning of mystical states. *International Review of Psycho-Analysis, 2*: 79–93.

Roth, P. (2001). *The Dying Animal.* Boston, MA: Houghton Mifflin.

Roth, P. (2006a). *Everyman.* Boston, MA: Houghton Mifflin.

Roth, P. (2006b). *Exit Ghost.* Boston, MA: Houghton Mifflin.

Rycroft, C. (1954). Review of G. Devereux (Ed.), "Psychoanalysis and the occult". *International Journal of Psychoanalysis, 35*: 70–71.

Sacks, O. (2015). *On the Move: A Life.* New York: Alfred A. Knopf.

Sadhguru (2012). What is surrender? https://youtube.com/watch?v=TMHhylNs-3Q (last accessed December 19, 2023).

Safran, J. D. (2016). Agency, surrender, and grace in psychoanalysis. *Psychoanalytic Psychology, 33*(1): 58–72.

Satran, G. (1991). Some limits and hazards of empathy. *Contemporary Psychoanalysis, 27*: 737–747.

Schaefer, R. (1959). Generative empathy in the treatment situation. *Psychoanalytic Quarterly, 28*: 342–373.

Schaefer, R. (1970). The psychoanalytic vision of reality. *International Journal of Psychoanalysis, 51*: 279–297.

Schinaia, C. (2019). Respect for the environment: Psychoanalytic reflections on the ecological crisis. *International Journal of Psychoanalysis, 100*: 272–286.

Searles, H. (1960). *The Nonhuman Environment in Normal Development and in Schizophrenia.* New York: International Universities Press.

Segal, L. (2013). *Out of Time: The Pleasures and Perils of Aging.* London: Verso.

Segall, M. H., Campbell, D. T., & Herskovits, M. J. (1966). *The Influence of Culture on Visual Perception.* Indianapolis, IN: Bobbs-Merrill.

Servadio, E. (1966). A psychodynamic approach to yoga experience. *International Journal of Parapsychology, 8*(2): 181–191.

Shafii, M. (1973). Silence in service of the ego: Psychoanalytic study of meditation. *International Journal of Psychoanalysis, 45*: 431–443.

Shankar, R. (n.d.). Quotes for life. http://anandway.com/quotes/gurudevsri-sri-ravi-shankar/Surrender (last accessed April 10, 2021).

Shankar, R. (2016). *Meaning of Surrender* and *Significance of Surrender.* https://youtube.com/watch?v=P0GOIAK8ces (last accessed October 3, 2022).

Shapiro, T. (1974). The development and distortions of empathy. *Psychoanalytic Quarterly, 43*: 4–25.

Shweder, R. A., & Haidt, J. (1993). The cultural psychology of emotions: Ancient and new. In: M. Lewis & J. M. Haviland-Jones (Eds.), *Handbook of Emotions* (pp. 379–414). New York: Guilford.

Silvan, M. (1981). Reply to Alan Roland's paper on "Psychoanalytic perspectives on personality development in India". *International Journal of Psychoanalysis*, 8: 93–99.

Sinha, T. C. (1966). Development of psychoanalysis in India. *International Journal of Psychoanalysis*, 47: 427–439.

Spence, D. P. (1986). Narrative smoothing and clinical wisdom. In: T. Sarbin (Ed.), *Narrative Psychology*. New York: Praeger.

Spence, D. P. (1988). Discussion of I. Moses: The misuse of empathy in psychoanalysis. *Contemporary Psychoanalysis*, 24: 594–598.

Spitz, R. (1957). *No and Yes*. New York: International Universities Press.

Sri Aurobindo (1911). Yogic Sadhan. *Sri Aurobindo Archives and Research* (1986) *10*(1): 55–83.

Steinmann, R. M. (1986). *Guru-Sisya-Sambandha: Das Meister-Schüler Verhältnis im traditionellen und modernen Hinduismus*. Stuttgart, Germany: Steiner.

Tagore, R. (n.d.). *Letter to C. F. Andrews*. Shantiniketan, India: Tagore Archives.

Tagore, R. (1913, October 11). *Letter to C. F. Andrews*. Shantiniketan, India: Tagore Archives.

Tagore, R. (1921). *Glimpses of Bengal*. New York: Macmillan.

Tagore, R. (1922). *Creative Unity*. London: Macmillan.

Tagore, R. (1938). *Prantik*. Shantiniketan, India: Visva-Bharati University Press.

Ticho, G. (1971). Cultural aspects of transference and countertransference. *Buletin of the Menninger Clinic*, *35*(5): 313–326.

Trapp, E. (2021). Unconsciousness rising: Sublimation and environmental loss. *Psychoanalysis, Culture & Society*, *26*: 65–83.

Tuch, R. (1997). Beyond empathy: Concerning certain complexities in the self psychology theory. *Psychoanalytic Quarterly*, *66*: 259–282.

UNICEF (2018). Infant and Young Child Feeding Data. *UNICEF*. https://data.unicef.org/resources/dataset/infant-young-child-feeding/ (last accessed May 9, 2020).

Updike, J. (1997). *Towards the End of Time*. New York: Random House.

Vaidyanathan, T. R., & Kripal, J. (1999). *Vishnu on Freud's Desk*. Delhi: Oxford University Press.

Vyasa (n.d.). *Mahabharata*. K. M. Ganguli (Trans.). Calcutta, India: Oriental Press.

Wagner, J. W. (2005). Psychoanalytic bias against the elderly patient: Hiding our fears under developmental millstones. *Contemporary Psychoanalysis*, *41*(1): 77–92.

Ward, I. (1993). Ecological madness, a Freud Museum conference: Introductory thoughts. *British Journal of Psychotherapy*, *10*: 178–187.

Weintrobe, S. (2009). On runaway greed and climate change denial: A psychoanalytic perspective. Lecture Series, *Psychotherapy in the 21st Century*. April 25, Lincoln Clinic & Centre for Psychotherapy, London.

Weintrobe, S. (2013). *Engaging with Climate Change: Psychoanalytic and Interdisciplinary Perspectives*. Hove: Routledge.

Werman, D. S. (1986). On the nature of the oceanic experience. *Journal of the American Psychoanalytic Association, 34*: 123–139.

Winnicott, D. W. (1965). The maturational processes and the facilitating environment. *Studies in the Theory of Emotional Development, 64*: 1.

Wylie, H. W., Jr., & Wylie, M. L. (1987). The older analysand: Counter-transference issues in psychoanalysis. *International Journal of Psychoanalysis, 68*: 343–352.

Yampey, N. (1989). Psicoanalysis de la cultura. *Revista de Psicoanalisis, 46*(3): 303–316.

Yeats, W. S. (1976). *Collected Poems*. New York: Macmillan.

Zweig, S. (1931). *Die Heilung durch den Geist. Mesmer, Mary Baker-Eddy, Freud*. Leipzig, Germany: Insel.

Index